Public Administration with an Attitude

H. George Frederickson

University of Kansas

American Society for Public Administration

*Advancing excellence
in public service . . .*

Published in 2005 in the United States of America by the American Society for Public Administration, 1120 G Street, NW, Suite 700, Washington, DC, 20005-3885. www.aspanet.org

Public Administration with an Attitude / H. George Frederickson
  Includes index
  ISBN 0-936678-24-0

Public Administration with an Attitude

H. George Frederickson

Table of Contents

Book Three: Real Public Administration Leaders

Book Four: Modern Public Organization and Management

Book Five: Public Administration as Reform

Acknowledgements

When John Larkin suggested that there might be an audience for a collection of some of the better columns I have written for PA TIMES, I quickly warmed to the idea. In the first place, I reasoned, most of the work had already been done. In the second place, I had recently completed two heavily academic projects, and the opportunity to do something lighter and more directly applied was welcome. In the third place, John suggested that the proposed book be a project of the American Society for Public Administration (ASPA), a wonderful professional association about which I care deeply. Having thus been drawn into it, the book project involved more work than I had anticipated. But that work was more enjoyable than I had imagined it might be. It was enjoyable in part because John Larkin is the kind of editor every author loves to work with — direct, upbeat, fast, and irreverent. My first and biggest thanks go, therefore, to John Larkin and to the good staff of ASPA.

For many years Christine Jewett McCrehin has been the particularly capable Editor-in-Chief of PA TIMES. It has been her job to hold me to publication deadlines, edit my work, and generally make my column as good as it is able to be. She carefully represents the sensitivities of PA TIMES readers and the purposes of ASPA and of PA TIMES. Above all she conveys the kind of trust that a columnist hopes for. I thank her for years of support and confidence.

Mary Hamilton was, for years, the Executive Director of ASPA and the Editor of PA TIMES. She was a continuing source of sound advice and good judgment. Over the years when she rejected columns it was always because they could have been interpreted as needlessly critical of the public service. She was right. Opinion columnists sometimes go too far. Mary helped keep me from these mistakes, for which I extend my thanks. Antoinette Samuel is the new Executive Director of ASPA. She too has been supportive and encouraging.

At the University of Kansas, Sabine Jones and Diana Koslowsky have patiently worked with me in processessing drafts, meeting deadlines, and helping me with the challenges or word processing. Far more important, they bring order, reliability and sunshine to the day-to-day work of the department of which I am a part. My colleagues and students at the Department of Public Administration are a steady source of new column ideas and a reliable sounding board for those ideas.

Above all I thank my wife Mary, who edited most of the columns before they appeared in PA TIMES. Those who aspire to a writing career would be wise to marry an English major. *Public Administration with an Attitude* is dedicated to her.

Book One
The Founders and the Founding
Concepts of Public Administration

Alexander Hamilton: Embrace Your Inner Federalist

The powerful linkages between Alexander Hamilton and American public administration were fully described decades ago by two of the leading scholars of the day. Lynton Keith Caldwell published *The Administrative Theories of Hamilton and Jefferson* in 1944, and in 1956 Leonard D. White published *The Federalists: A Study of Administrative History*. Unfortunately both books are long out-of-print, available now only in the best of libraries. Both of these excellent studies describe the affinity between the philosophical position of the Federalists, and particularly Hamilton, and the intellectual underpinnings of modern public administration. Indeed more recently Vincent Ostrom argued that Hamilton, rather than Woodrow Wilson ought properly to be thought of as the father of American public administration. And finally the eminent contemporary scholar Donald Kettl claims that American public administration is essentially Hamiltonian in philosophy whereas political science, often thought of as the mother discipline of public administration, is essentially Madisonian.

Let me digress briefly to describe Hamilton in more human terms, because his was the quintessential American story. He was born in St. Croix in the Carribean, the illegitimate son of James Hamilton, an itinerant Scot, and Rachel Faucett, of Huguenot decent. Prior to meeting Hamilton, Rachel Faucett had been jailed for declining to live with her husband. Although still married, she and Hamilton had two sons, James and Alexander. Not long after Alexander was born, his father left. Rachel owned a provisions store in St. Croix to support her children. Alexander was bright, had good early schooling and at an early age was apprenticed as a clerk to a merchant-trader. He sailed alone and with virtually no money to New York when he was fourteen. He worked as a clerk, put himself through Kings College, now Columbia University, and read the law. He was a hero of the Revolutionary War, serving as one of Washington's primary aides. At age thirty-two he was appointed Secretary of the Treasury in Washington's first cabinet and served throughout Washington's first term. It is generally agreed that Hamilton's organization of the Department of Treasury was fundamentally important to the early stability and effectiveness of American government. He took accounts that were in shambles and put them in order, he balanced the books, he paid off the Revolutionary War debt and he built the foundation for what is now the Federal Reserve Bank.

Compared to the Virginian aristocracy—Washington, Madison, Monroe, and Jefferson, and the high-born of Boston, John and John Quincy Adams—Hamilton's may be the most compelling American story.

His story and his remarkable service to his country are less important than his words. More than any other Founder, he shaped the Federalist perspective, and that perspective has always shaped American public administration. Here are some of his words and ideas.

On the Powers of Government:

"A government ought to contain ... every power requisite to the ... accomplishment of the objects committed to its care, and to the complete execution of the trusts for which it is responsible, free from every other control but regard to the public good and to the sense of the people."

On the Executive Branch:

"Energy in the executive is a leading character in the definition of good government. It is essential ... to the steady administration of the laws, to the protection of property against ... irregular and high-handed combinations,... to the security of liberty against the enterprises ... of faction."

"The vigor of government" is "essential to the security of liberty."

"When the dimensions of a State attain to a certain magnitude, it requires the same energy of government ... which [is] requisite in one of much greater extent.... The citizens of America have too much discernment to be argued into anarchy. And ... experience has ... wrought a deep ... conviction ... that greater energy of government is essential to the welfare ... of the community."

"[T]he true test of a good government is its aptitude and tendency to produce a good administration."

An energetic executive is necessary "to the protection of property against those irregular and high-handed combinations [factions] which sometimes interrupt the ordinary course of justice; to the security of liberty against the enterprises and assaults of ambition, of faction, and of anarchy."

On the Legislative Branch:

"The tendency of the legislative authority to absorb every other, has been fully displayed.... In governments purely republican, this tendency is almost irresistible."

"[T]he representatives ... in a popular assembly seem sometimes to fancy that they are the people themselves, and betray strong symptoms of impatience and disgust at the least sign of opposition from any other quarter; as if the exercise of rights, by either the executive or judiciary, were a breach of their privilege and an outrage to their dignity. They often appear disposed to exert an imperious control over the other departments; and as they commonly have the people on their side, they always act with such momentum as to make it very difficult for the other members of the government to maintain the balance of the Constitution."

On the Judicial Branch:

"The independence of the judges is ... requisite to guard ... the rights of individuals from the effects of those ill humors, which the arts of designing men, or the influence of particular conjectures, sometimes disseminate among the people ... and which ... have a tendency ... to occasion ... serious oppressions of the minor party."

"[T]he interpretation of the laws is the proper and peculiar province of the courts."

The courts must "do their duty as faithful guardians of the

Constitution, where legislative invasions of it had been instituted by the major voice of the community."

On Direct Democracy:

"It has been observed that a pure democracy, if it were practicable, would be the most perfect government. Experience has proven that no position in politics is more false than this. The ancient democracies (Greece and Italy), in which the people themselves deliberated, never possessed one feature of good government. Their very character was tyranny; their figure deformity. When they assembled, the field of debate presented an ungovernable mob, not only incapable of deliberation, but prepared for every enormity. In these assemblies the enemies of the people brought forward their plans of ambition systematically. They were opposed by their enemies of another party; and ... the people subjected themselves to be led blindly by one tyrant or by another."

On Federalism and States Rights:

"If a number of political societies enter into a larger political society, the laws which the latter may enact, pursuant to the powers entrusted to it by its constitution, must necessarily be supreme over those societies, and the individuals of whom they are composed. It would otherwise be a mere treaty, dependent on the good faith of the parties, and not a government, which is only another word for political power and supremacy."

Hamilton complains of "those practices ... of the State governments which have undermined the foundations of property and credit, have planted mutual distrust in the breasts of all classes of citizens, and have occasioned an almost universal prostration of morals."

On the Separation of Powers and Checks and Balances:

"But a confederacy of the people, without exaggeration, may be said to be entirely the masters of their own fate. Power being almost always the rival of power, the general government will at all times stand ready to check the usurpations of the state governments, and these will have the same disposition towards the general government. The people, by throwing themselves into either scale, will infallibly make use of the other as the instruments of redress."

9

"It is a fundamental maxim of free government, that the three great departments of power, legislative, executive, and judiciary, shall be essentially distinct and independent, the one of the other."

"A salutary check upon the legislative body, calculated to guard the community against the effects of faction, precipitancy, or of any impulse unfriendly to the public good, which may happen to influence a majority of that body."

I recently visited Alexander Hamilton where he is buried in the yard of Trinity Church in lower Manhattan a few blocks from the site of the World Trade Center. Hamilton, more than any of the founders with the possible exception of Benjamin Franklin, saw clearly what the United States was to become. And Hamilton was the only founder with a well-developed understanding of what was to become public administration. So, I thought he might have useful opinions on contemporary American affairs.

First, I asked, "How shall the national government respond to the destruction of the World Trade Center and to terrorism generally?"

"Well, in the first place," Hamilton replied, "a full and reasoned response to terrorism requires, as I wrote as Publius, 'energy in the executive.... [It] is the definition of good government. It is essential to the protection of the community against foreign attack. It is not less essential to the steady administration of the laws, to the protection of property against those irregular and high-handed combinations, which sometime interrupt the ordinary course of justice to the security of liberty against the enterprises and assaults of ambition, of faction and of anarchy.' It appears to me," Hamilton continued, "that the overall response of the national government to the attack on the World Trade Center had all of the characteristics of energy in the executive."

"Well," I replied, "although we have had some support from other nations, particularly Great Britain, much of the international response to the bombing of the World Trade Center has been primarily by the United States. Is that a wise course of action?"

"I must confess," Hamilton answered, "that it appears that the American response to terrorism and to other contemporary international matters, shows evidence of a lack of trust in alliances. This is a mistake.

I wrote as Publius that 'there is nothing absurd or impractical in the idea of a league or alliance between independent nations, for certain defined purposes precisely stated in a treaty; regulating all the details of time, place, circumstances, and quantity,... depending for its execution on the good faith of the parties. Compacts of this kind exist among all civilized nations subject to the usual vicissitudes of peace and war, of observance and non-observance, as the interests and passions of the contracting powers dictate.' It seems to me that this is a time calling for the highest of diplomatic skills. Our leaders should be everywhere busy building anti-terrorism treaties and alliances, not only for purposes of anti-terrorism, but for purposes of the mutual multi-state regulation of business practices. We have just begun what will someday be thought of as the global century, and the United States should lead the development of global responses to global problems. However strong we are and however right we are, in the longer run we cannot go it alone," Hamilton replied.

I then asked, "The law which established the Department of Homeland Security includes provisions which would limit the civil service protections of staff members and provide for what the administration believes to be greater bureaucratic responsiveness. What do you think of those proposals?"

"The elements of 'energy in the executive are first, unity, secondly duration, thirdly, an adequate provision for its support, and fourthly competent powers,'" Hamilton replied. "In good administration 'unity may be destroyed in two ways: either by vesting the power in two or more magistrates of equal dignity and authority; or by vesting it ostensibly in one man, subject in whole or in part to the control and co-operation of others.' Establishing a department and a secretary for homeland security satisfies the requirement for unity.

"As to duration, there is a serious flaw in the design of the Department of Homeland Security because too many top officials are politically appointed. The administrative staff of a magistrate, or as you would say, secretary, should have some permanence and protection because, as I wrote as Publius, the administrative staff is continually beset 'by the wiles of parasites and sycophants, by the snares of the very ambitious, the avaricious, the desperate; by the artifices of men who possess their confidence more than they deserve it. When occasions present themselves in which the interests of the people are at variance with their inclinations, it is the duty of the persons who have been appointed the guardians of those interests, to withstand the temporary delusion, in order to give them time and opportunity for more cool and sedate reflection. Instances might be cited, in which a conduct of this kind has saved the people from very fatal consequences of their own mistakes, and has procured lasting monuments of their gratitude to the men, who had the courage and magnanimity enough to serve them at the peril of their own displeasure.' It is for these reasons that there must always be a permanent, professional, and protected civil service particularly in a field as sensitive as homeland security. The permanent administration holds the best prospects for protecting the people and their representatives from their own excesses."

"Mr. Hamilton," I said, "to change the subject, what do you think of congressional decisions that have increased support for American agriculture and decreased support for child welfare?"

"They have it exactly backwards," he said. "First, the needs of poor children cannot be met by voluntary contributions. You may recall the closing paragraph in my *Report on Manufactures* which reads, 'In countries where there is great private wealth much may be effected by the voluntary contributions of patriotic individuals, but in a community situated like that of the United States, the public purse must supply the deficiency of private resource.' Second, it is always a mistake for the government to subsidize the economy. Earlier in the *Report on Manufactures* I wrote, 'To endeavor by the extraordinary patronage of the government to accelerate the growth of manufactures is in fact, to endeavor, by force and art, to transfer the natural current of industry from a more, to a less beneficial channel.... Indeed it can hardly ever be wise in a government, to attempt to give a direction to the industry of its citizens.... To leave industry to itself therefore, is, in almost every case, the soundest as well as the simplest policy.' As you will recall, I argue elsewhere in the *Report* that the relationship between government and industry should be the same as the relationship between government and agriculture."

"How, then, do we account for the policies which reduce child welfare support and increase agriculture support? Is Congress simply irrational?" I asked. Mr. Hamilton replied, "Ah, my young friend, you have stumbled into the right question. The answer is factions, or as you now call them, special interests, although I must say I find nothing particularly special about them. In my speech on interests and corruption given to the convention called in New York state to consider ratifying the draft Constitution, I said that there was 'in the conduct of members of Congress a strong and uniform attachment to the interests of their own state. These interests have, on many occasions, been adhered to, with an undue and illiberal pertinacity, and have too often been preferred to the welfare of the Union.' So, it is the power of special interests and the tendency of members of Congress to favor the interests of their own states over the general public good that accounts for increasing subsidies to agriculture and declining support for children in poverty. You will recall that as Publius I warned that 'a spirit of faction which is apt to mingle its poison in the deliberations of all bodies of men, will often hurry the persons to whom they are composed into improprieties and excesses, for which they would blush in a private capacity.' At a minimum, members of Congress should blush over their subsidies to agriculture."

"Well, Mr. Hamilton, it has been a pleasure to visit with you again," I said. "Do you have any parting advice?"

"Yes," he said, "stick with that policy-administration dichotomy thing. All true Federalists really like the dichotomy."

As the sharpness of these words attest, Alexander Hamilton was an impolitic man. But of all the Founders, it is Hamilton who saw most clearly what the United States of America could become. And it was Hamilton who built the foundation for what would become professional public administration. Although he has long been out of fashion, let me suggest that in most respects we are all Hamiltonians.

Max Weber and George, Together at Last

While visiting in Europe recently I decided to go to Heidelberg to see if the inventor of bureaucracy, Max Weber, would give me an interview. Well, Weber did not actually invent bureaucracy, but he certainly did describe it in detail.

Fortunately he was available and willing to see me. Upon entering his office I said: "Dr. Weber, it is a great honor to finally meet you."

"Yes, young fellow," he said, "it is an honor for you to meet me, inasmuch as many people in your country think I am dead."

"That's true," I said, "but it may be just wishful thinking."

He sat behind a desk that was clean save for a little alabaster paperweight carved in the shape of a pyramid. His office was bright and orderly, although I did notice an unusual number of filing cabinets and bureaus along one wall. Weber is tall, solidly built, with a full head of pure white hair; the total impression is of command, physical authority, and charisma.

"Yes," he said. "It suits some people to think that I am dead, in much the same way that some think bureaucracy is dead."

"Well, Dr. Weber," I said, "it may not be that they think bureaucracy is dead. It may be that they are out to kill it."

"Call me Max," he said. "Yes, I have read that stuff about the bankruptcy of bureaucracy and about banishing bureaucracy."

"Well, Max, we do have serious problems with bureaucracy, not only in my country but in many countries," I said. "People are sick and tired of rigid, bloated, self-serving, unimaginative, risk-averse bureaucracies that lack compassion."

"Take it easy, George, you are beginning to sound like someone from a management consulting firm," he said. "Are the people who are tired of problems of bureaucracy equally tired of the stability, order, and reliably predictable service they receive from government? Are they equally tired of the highly favorable environment in which the giant American corporate machine functions, an environment made possible by laws and regulations and by the bureaucrats that implement those laws and regulations?"

"Gee, Max, you are some fancy talker," I said. "No, the people, and particularly their political representatives, want the stability and order that bureaucracy brings without all of the expensive baggage that comes with it. You are the world's greatest scholar of bureaucracy, Max, tell me how we can have the good of bureaucracy without the bad?"

"Ach, mein junger Dummkopf!" he replied. "Are there no graduate schools in America? Are you sure you studied public administration?"

Stunned by his sharp reply, I was silent.

Realizing that I was hurt, Weber then said, "Perhaps you need a brief tutorial."

"Long before you were born I wrestled with this vexing problem in both *The Protestant Ethic and the Spirit of Capitalism* and in *The Theory of Social and Economic Organization.* I wrote: 'No country and no age has ever experienced, in the same sense as the modern Occident, the absolute and complete dependence of its whole existence, of the political, technical, and economic conditions of its life, on a specially trained organization of officials.' These are the bureaucrats and it is their bureaucracies that make possible the political, technical, and economic conditions of all advanced countries. In all of their efficient impersonal rationality, these bureaucracies are also, I wrote, iron cages. Almost 100 years ago—now I am giving away my age—I described this paradox in your country, my young friend. 'In the field of its (bureaucracy's) highest development, in the United States, the pursuit of wealth, stripped of its religious and ethical meaning, tends to become associated with purely mundane passions, which often actually give it the character of sport.'"

"Boy, you sure got that right Max," I said. "Where will this lead?"

"No one knows who will live in this cage in the future or whether at the end of this tremendous development there will emerge entirely new prophets with new ideas or there will instead be a great rebirth of old ideas and ideals or neither, resulting in mechanized petrification, embellished with a sort of convulsive self-importance."

"Well," I responded, "in the United States we have had many

claiming to be new prophets of public administration, but almost all of them call for greater efficiency, greater rationality, and greater productivity. A few advocate greater compassion and the more equitable distribution of both government services and educational and career opportunities, but few listen to them. It is the efficiency prophets who are listened to in the halls of political power. And you are right again, Max, they do display a kind of 'convulsive self-importance.'"

Then showing a dazzling knowledge of contemporary scholarship, Weber said: "I even see good evidence of what I called 'mechanized petrification' discovered by two fine young American scholars, Paul DiMaggio and Walter Powell. As you know, in their study of many large bureaucracies including corporations, governments, and universities, they found what they call 'institutional isomorphism.' Under conditions of goal ambiguity, resource dependency, and technical uncertainty, conditions that pertain to almost all governments, big institutions will mimic and copy each other to the point that they come to look and act about the same. So, big bureaucracies do not in fact pursue differentiation in search of efficiency so much as they pursue similarity in search of acceptance and prestige. It seems to me that institutional isomorphism is my prediction of 'mechanized petrification' come true."

"Well," I replied, "You are probably right. Xerox won the Baldridge Prize a few years back and now you have to practically give their stock away. But Max, you still have not told me how to reconcile the benefits and costs of bureaucracy."

"This may surprise you, George, given my reputation, but I would recommend certain bureaucratic reforms. First, the bureaucracy should worry less about a generalized efficiency and worry much more about who in society is benefiting and who is losing as a result of the pursuit of generalized efficiency. The question is not whether a bureaucracy is efficient, the question should be, 'for whom is the bureaucracy efficient?' Even the most democratic country will not endure if there is an extensive and growing gap between the haves and the have nots. Second, stop worrying about the fact that bureaucrats have power. No informed person really believes that bureaucrats are neutral anyway.

The ministerial functions of government always have power and that power should be exercised not just in the service of commerce but also in the service of the whole people. Third, have passion in the pursuit of good government and equal passion to resist ideas that are harmful to government and especially to people. Remember, I wrote long ago that we need to worry that bureaucrats often become 'specialists without spirit, and sensualists without heart.' So, the key to reconciling the good and the bad in bureaucracy will not be found in an exaggerated search for greater efficiency. It will be found in the spirit and heart of good bureaucrats and their bureaucracies."

"Wow, Max, that sounds like a Sunday School lesson."

"Call it whatever you like, George."

Later, on the train leaving Heidelberg, I resolved to take more seriously the early literature of public administration. I also remembered that Weber was not only the first great scholar of bureaucracy, he was also a leading student of world religions. And, I decided to take him up on his invitation to call on him again.

Herbert Simon and Dwight Waldo: Truly the Giants of Public Administration

Herbert Simon and Dwight Waldo were two giants astride the second half of twentieth century American public administration. To practice or theorize about modern public administration is to have been influenced by Simon and Waldo. Simon, the Nobel laureate, was the father of decision theory, operations research, and bounded rationality. He saw clearly the coming of the information age and he systematically molded and shaped it. Waldo was the father of most modern conceptions of bureaucratic politics. He saw clearly the political and philosophical issues facing what he rightly called the emergence of the administrative state.

Both are now gone.

To put the importance of Simon and Waldo in perspective it is useful to return to the middle of the twentieth century and to the beginnings of their careers. Both found the policy-administration dichotomy, and the "principles of public administration" as represented by POSD-CORB faulty. Both had reservations about the claims of neutrality associated with a merit-based civil service. Both understood that a public administration based primarily on the progressive-reform era drive to stamp out government corruption and spoils and to get politics out of administration was not an adequate conceptual foundation for this new field. At mid-century both knew that the future of American public administration would not look like the past. Where they differed had to do with what the future of public administration would look like. And they didn't differ just a little.

To understand those differences, it is necessary to go back to their mid-century debate. Sad to say, that debate is now seldom read. But it is a powerful presentation of the contrasting epistemologies of the two most powerful minds in the field. In 1952 Waldo wrote a long essay in *American Political Science Review* for the very first issue of the year, titled "Development of Theory of Democratic Administration," which reviewed much of the public administration literature of the time, including Simon's *Administrative Behavior*. In condensed form, here is what Waldo wrote:

—One major obstacle in the way of further development of democratic theory is the idea that efficiency is a value-neutral concept or, still worse, that it is antithetical to democracy. To hold that we should take efficiency as the central concept of our "science" but that we nevertheless must tolerate a certain amount of democracy because we "believe" in it is to poison the taproot of American society. To maintain that efficiency is value-neutral and to propose at the same time that it be used as the central concept in a "science" of administration is to commit one's self to nihilism, so long as the prescription is actually followed.

—Efficiency is, however, a tenet of orthodoxy that has refused to decline. No one now believes in any strict separation of politics and administration; but in the proposition that there are "value decisions" and "factual decisions" and that the latter can be made in terms of efficiency.

—In this contention, the present "weight of authority" is against me. But I believe that there is no realm of "factual decisions" from which values are excluded. To decide is to choose between alternatives; to choose between alternatives is to introduce values. Herbert Simon has patently made outstanding contributions to administrative study. These contributions have been made, however, when he has worked free of the methodology he has asserted.

In the very next issue Simon replied. His response is reproduced here in condensed form:

—Since Dwight Waldo has credited me with "contributions" to public administration, I suppose that I might be flattered rather than dismayed by his treatment of the fact-value issue in his recent article.

—A scientist is not (and, in my system of personal values, should not be) flattered by being told that his conclusions are good, but do not follow from his premises. If Mr. Waldo's footnote 40, on page 97, is correct, then I should be condemned, not flattered.

—Study of logic and empirical science has impressed on me the extreme care that must be exercised, in the search for truth, to avoid logical booby traps. For this reason the kind of prose I encounter in writings on political theory, decorated with assertion, invective, and metaphor, sometimes strikes me as aesthetically pleasing, but seldom as convincing.

—No one who has studied seriously the writings of logical positivists, or my own discussion of fact and value in *Administrative Behavior*, could attribute to us the "proposition that there are 'value decisions' and 'factual decisions.'"

—Quite apart from whether Mr. Waldo's premises are right or wrong, I do not see how we can progress in political philosophy if we continue to think and write in the loose, literary, metaphorical style that he and most other political theorists adopt. The standard of unrigor that is tolerated in political theory would not receive a passing grade in the elementary course in logic, Aristotelian or symbolic.

To this Waldo then replied, again in condensed form:

—Professor Simon charges me with profaning the sacred places of Logical Positivism, and I am afraid I have. I use this figure of speech because Professor Simon seems to me that rare individual in our secular age, a man of deep faith. His convictions are monolithic and massive. His toleration of heresy and sin is nil. The Road to Salvation is straight, narrow, one-way, and privately owned. We must humbly confess our sins, accept the Word, be washed pure in the Blood of Carnap and Ayer. Then, he says, we will no longer be "enemies."

—Even if we should be inclined to elect salvation by logical positivism, the matter is not so simple as it is represented by Professor Simon.

—May I state for the record, though I had hoped that I had made it clear, that I am not opposed to positivism and empiricism as whole bodies of thought or techniques of investigation or action.

—The creative processes of the mind are still a mystery and at best are merely aided by training in logic, Professor Simon must know. Perhaps Professor Simon needs to examine whether the logical positivism of which he is enamored has become an obstacle in his pursuit of the science to which he is dedicated. To me, at least, logical positivism, empiricism, and science are far from being the nearly or wholly congruent things which they seem to be to Professor Simon.

If there were prophets in public administration, there would be the Book of Simon and the Book of Waldo and these words would be our scripture.

In the decades that followed, both Simon and Waldo would build their respective perspectives on the field, each leaving an impressive body of scholarship. Over the years both mellowed and tended to express their views with less certitude. Although representing very different epistemologies, they developed great respect for one another. Waldo sent congratulations to him when Simon was given the Waldo Award by the American Society for Public Administration. In his acceptance speech, Simon said how proud he was to have received the Waldo award, how much his later work had been influenced by Waldo, and how much he respected him.

Today, public administration is still science and art, facts and values, Hamilton and Jefferson, politics and administration, Simon and Waldo. Some call for a grand and overarching theory "which would bring the field together." For my tastes, public administration is now very much together in all its complexity, a complexity richly and forever informed by Herbert Simon and Dwight Waldo.

How I Became A Waldonian

D wight Waldo died.

The book, *The Study of Public Administration*, by Dwight Waldo was published in 1955 by Doubleday. It cost 95 cents in 1962, less than a penny a page. There was just one printing and it was out-of-print by the late 1960s. The contentious debate between Waldo and Simon is essential, and Waldo's seminal but dense *Administrative State* is fundamental to public administration. But, it was *The Study of Public Administration* that breathed life into the scholarly field of public administration. In it Waldo carefully defined the field, including public administration as art and science, public administration as rational action and as nonrational action, and the meaning of public in public administration. He carefully traced the history, evolution and development of the academic field of public administration, making careful distinctions between the practice of public administration and its study. Waldo reviewed the teaching of the subject, including a special emphasis on the case method and the importance of texts. He then systematically connected the practice and study of public administration to the social sciences in a wonderfully interdisciplinary way. Finally, befitting his view of the field, he closed with a thoughtful treatment of what he called "the value problem in administrative study."

Although scholarship, research and theory in public administration have advanced significantly in the nearly fifty years since Waldo wrote *The Study of Public Administration*, for my tastes there has never been a better book on the subject.

Imagine my good fortune to be Dwight Waldo's colleague at the Maxwell School of Citizenship and Public Affairs at Syracuse University. The words "awe," "veneration," "esteem," or "respect" come close to how I felt, but all are weak. Dwight, however, was unpretentious, gracious, and particularly generous to me and to his other junior colleagues and to our collective students. The last thing he wanted was to be held in awe. The first thing he wanted was a good lively discussion of the subject he knew so well and so obviously loved.

Dwight was a living bridge to the distinguished origins of American public administration. He knew and worked with many of the great names of the early years of modern public administration—John Gaus, Paul Appleby, both William Mosher and Dwight's dearest friend Frederick "Fritz" Mosher, Leonard White, Robert Dahl, Charles Lindblom, Herbert Simon, Luther Gulick, Harold Stein, Catherine Seckler-Hudson, V.O. Key, Harvey Mansfield, John Millett, Don Price, Don Stone, Wallace Sayre, and Mary Parker Follet. He took history seriously and could always be counted on to identify early works that touched on modern approaches thought to be unique or new. Yet he was relentlessly encouraging of young scholars and new ideas and somewhat impatient with attempts to dismiss new ideas with claims that they were just new wine in old bottles. This example comes to mind. In the early 1970s, as schools of policy analysis and policy study were replacing public administration programs at many leading American universities, some faculty in public administration schools and programs were rather dismissive of this movement. Dwight would patiently say: "There is something important in the policy studies approach. You would be wise not to dismiss it. You would be wise to embrace it. Think of it as public administration in another language." He was right. Policy schools and the policy approach did become very important. And the recent evidence is that the policy schools and the public administration schools, while using somewhat different languages, are looking more and more alike. Waldo was right again.

And now he is gone.

Dwight, through his students, was also a bridge forward, to the future. Several present-day scholars and leaders in public administration were his students—Ken Meier, Larry O'Toole, Tom Lauth, Charles Washington, Jim Carroll, Walter Broadnax, Richard Stillman, Brack Brown, David Porter, Frank Marini, Astrid Merget, Donna Shalala, Glenn Hahn Cope and many others. And all of the MPA students who passed through the Maxwell School in those years were influenced if not directly as a student, indirectly by his presence.

During his Maxwell years Dwight also served for ten years as Editor-in-Chief of *Public Administration Review*, longer than anyone before or since. In those years there were few journals in the field and *PAR* stood alone as the voice of the field, powerfully influential in both the practice and study of public administration. Waldo's very high personal standards of scholarship carried over into the pages of *PAR*, lifting the overall quality of the journal. As a rookie scholar I certainly understood that *PAR* expected one's very best work and that Waldo stood at the head, an icon of standards.

In 1977, when Dwight decided that ten years as *PAR* Editor-in-Chief were enough, it fell to me as President of ASPA that year, to appoint his successor. There were excellent candidates. Finally, after the good work of a screening committee, I decided on Lewis Gawthrop. When I called him extending ASPA's invitation to serve as the editor of *PAR*, the very first thing he said was: "How can I ever fill Dwight's shoes?" He filled Dwight's shoes very well indeed as have the *PAR* editors who followed—Chet Newland, David Rosenbloom, Irene Rubin, Larry Terry, and Richard Stillman. But even today it is clear that it was Waldo who set the standard for what ASPA and the entire field of public administration expects of the *PAR* editor. It was entirely befitting that ASPA and *PAR* decided to name the annual prize for "distinguished contributions to the professional literature of public administration," the Dwight Waldo Award.

In 1997, over 100 of Waldo's students, friends and colleagues returned to the Maxwell School for a festschrift called The Waldo Symposium. It was a glorious two-and-one-half days of first class scholarship, wonderful reminiscences, toasts and good fellowship. The festschrift papers later appeared in *PAR* and in *JPART*. Dwight came up from Northern Virginia where he lived in retirement. He had a wonderful time and his little handwritten notes (we called them Waldograms) came through the mail to symposium participants for months afterward.

New copies of *The Administrative State* were available at the Waldo Symposium, and Dwight graciously autographed a copy for each of us along with a personal note. On mine he wrote a note, which is precious to me. And, at the bottom of the title page he also wrote these words: "Not Authentic Without This Signature. Dwight Waldo." Then he handed it to me with a little smile and a twinkle in his eye. It was a delightful example of Dwight's unique sense of humor.

My old copy of *The Study of Public Administration* made me a Waldonian forever. In many ways we are all Waldonians. To study public administration today is to have been influenced by Dwight Waldo. To do research in public administration today is to have been influenced by Dwight Waldo. To practice public administration today is to have been influenced by Dwight Waldo. Dwight will always be with us.

Harlan Cleveland: The Prophet of Public Administration

Of the many great contemporary leaders of the practice and theory of public administration, one stands out as our modern prophet. It is said that to prophesy the future one must have a deep knowledge of the past. Descriptions of the truly prophetic use traditional words like "wisdom" or "judgment," or cute modern phrases like "the ability to see around the corner." Above all, however, prophetic qualities rest on the prophet having been right regarding the future. The need for a prophetic track record is the reason why the real prophets still among us are, as we say, senior.

Our modern prophet is Harlan Cleveland.

In his explanation of "how I got here," Cleveland traces a life uniquely connected to many of the key events of the last 70 years. He was a schoolboy in the turmoil of Europe in the early 1930s, then a student at Princeton, then a Rhodes Scholarship at Oxford cut short when Hitler marched into Poland in 1939. Unable to serve in the military because of a bad eye, Cleveland worked on the civilian side of the war effort, ending up in 1944 with important responsibilities for restoring democracy in Italy, first for the U.S. government and later for the United Nations Relief and Rehabilitation Administration. He then took successive positions of responsibility in the U.S. Economic Cooperation Administration, the predecessor to the Agency for International Development, first for Asia and then for Europe. Then, in a dizzying succession of experiences he was editor of *The Reporter*, Dean of the Maxwell School at Syracuse University, head of the bureau dealing with multilateral diplomacy in the State Department in the Kennedy administration, ambassador to NATO in the Johnson administration, president of the University of Hawaii, head of the Program in International Affairs of the Aspen Institute, dean of the Humphrey School at the University of Minnesota and, finally, president of the World Academy of Art and Science. Cleveland is now retired, living with his wife Lois in Sterling, Virginia, still very busy working out of his home office, much of that work being done on the Internet.

Such a wide range of experiences over such a long period of time should, by themselves, suggest that Harlan Cleveland is worth listening to. To understand Cleveland's prophetic qualities, however, one must turn to his writings: 13 books and eight edited collections in the past 55 years. Of these books, to my tastes, the most prophetic is *The Future Executive: A Guide for Tomorrow's Managers*, published in 1972. Certainly *The Future Executive* was an important book in its time, but only now are we able to understand how prophetic it was.

Cleveland's description of contemporary public organizations is on the money. "The organizations that get things done will no longer be hierarchical pyramids with most of the real control at the top. They will be systems—interlaced webs of tension in which control is loose, power diffused, and centers of decision plural. 'Decision-making' will become an increasingly intricate process of multilateral brokerage both inside and outside the organization which thinks it has the responsibility for making, or at least announcing, the decision. Because organizations will be horizontal, the way they are governed is likely to be more collegial, consensual, and consultative. The bigger the problems to be tackled, the more real power is diffused and the larger the number of persons who can exercise it—if they work at it."

Like many, Cleveland saw the blurring of the distinctions between public and private organizations. He reasoned through what it meant as follows: "These new style public-private horizontal systems will be led by a new breed of men and women. I call them public executives, people who manage public responsibilities whether in 'public' or 'private' organizations."

It was Cleveland who first used the words "governing" and "governance" as surrogates for the public administration he saw coming. In the mid-1970s I distinctly remember a speech given at an annual meeting of ASPA in which he said this: "What the people want is less government and more governance." At the time I was somewhat skeptical, because the traditions of public administration had been tied so tightly to the functioning of formal governmental jurisdictions. Looking back it is clear that Cleveland, as we say, nailed it. "Governance" is now the dominant word/concept in the field, the way we describe forms of horizontal interorganizational cooperation. Cleveland, it could be argued, is the father of governance.

"Governance" is an especially important word/concept because of the mismatch or disconnect between jurisdictions on one hand and social, technological, political and economic problems on the other hand. Cleveland understood this too. "One of the striking ironies of our time is that, just when we have to build bigger, more complicated 'bundles of relations' to deal comprehensively with the human consequences of science and technology, many people are seized with the idea that large-scale organization is itself a bad thing. My thesis is the reverse." Big problems, Cleveland believes, require big responses. Those responses will, however, be multi-organizational and will involve both public and private organizations. These responses will, post Cleveland, be led by not one, but many leaders.

Cleveland clearly understood the challenges of individual accountability associated with multi-organizational systems. Who, exactly, do these modern public executives work for and to whom are they accountable? Consider this remarkably bold argument. "Public ethics are in the hearts and minds of individual public executives, and the ultimate court of appeals from their judgments is some surrogate for people-in-general." He does not argue that accountability is ultimately to the people or the elected officials of one's jurisdiction. Cleveland's idea of public responsibility is much bigger than that. The moral responsibility of public executives includes basic considerations of four fundamental principles: "a sense of welfare; a sense of equity; a sense of achievement; and a sense of participating."

What would be the results of such a grand conception of the moral responsibility of the public administrator? "In a society characterized by bigness and complexity, it is those individuals who learn to get things done in organizational systems who will have a rational basis for feeling free.... By the development of their administrative skills, and by coming squarely to terms with the moral requirements of executive leadership, individual men and women can preserve and extend their freedom. Freedom is the power to choose, and the future executive will be making the most choices—whom to bring together in which organizations, to make what happen, in whose interpretation of the public interest. Those who relish that role will have every reason to feel free, not in the interstices but right in the middle of things."

Harlan Cleveland is still the public administration prophet for our times. His predictions about the future of our field are in his latest book, *Nobody in Charge: Essays on the Future of Leadership*.

A Weber for Our Time: The Life and Work of Fred W. Riggs

Max Weber may be the father of comparison in public administration, but Fred W. Riggs is its most distinguished contemporary practitioner. Forty years before Benjamin Barber published *Jihad vs. McWorld* or Thomas Friedman published *The Lexus and the Olive Tree*,

Fred Riggs compared modern and premodern countries and discovered that no words were adequate to describe what he found. So he simply invented the needed words. In the Riggsian lexicon traditional or premodern states are "agraria," modern states are "industria" and states that combine elements of both are "prismatic societies." Using these categories Riggs brilliantly describes premodern, post-colonial developing countries and compares them to modern counties. In doing so he, like Weber, keeps a particularly keen eye on bureaucracies. Riggs' descriptions of prismatic societies are powerfully useful in our present circumstances and could serve to inform both policy makers and scholars. But I get ahead of the story.

Fred Riggs' life and work are verification of the claim that comparison is the beginning of knowledge, for he seems to have been destined to compare. He was born in China in 1917, the son of an American agricultural engineer who was there initially to advise the Chinese on experimental farming and later to serve as a faculty member in the first department of agricultural engineering in China, at the University of Nanking. With the exception of one year in the United States, Fred's primary education was in China. He learned an early lesson in development administration when it became clear to his father that most American agricultural techniques were irrelevant to the Chinese situation. Indeed, his father changed from advising the Chinese to learning ancient agricultural techniques from them.

China was in chaos during this period. Although there was an internationally recognized government in Beijing, most political power was in the hands of regional war lords. Two forces for political consolidation were in bloody competition, the Nationalists led by Chaing Kai Shek and the Communists led by Mao Tse Tung. When he was a schoolboy, Fred saw slain soldiers in the streets of Shaowu. After a year at the University of Nanking, in 1935 he enrolled at the University of Illinois, where, although he was an American, he experienced the culture shock of actually living in America. While he was at Illinois he took an American politics course from Charles Hyneman, and changed his major from journalism to political science. He graduated in 1938 with a Phi Beta Kappa key and was accepted by the Fletcher School of Law and Diplomacy at Tufts University, where he completed an M.A. in 1941. He was then accepted to the doctoral program in political science at Columbia University, but his studies were interrupted by the Japanese attack on Pearl Harbor and the onset of World War II. Following his family's beliefs, he declared himself to be a conscientious objector and, unable to secure a posting as an ambulance driver in China, was assigned to a domestic civilian public service program operated by the Quakers. After the war he returned to Columbia and finished his dissertation, a study of the repeal of the racist Chinese Exclusion Acts, later published as *Pressures on Congress*. Among his findings was evidence of the influence of key bureaucrats at both the State Department and the Bureau of the Budget in the push for repeal. This was also evidence of a commitment on the part of certain upper level bureaucrats to social equity.

For the next six years Fred worked for several organizations that were engaged in research and technical assistance. Their work was primarily associated with developing countries, particularly Ethiopia, Formosa, and Korea. In 1957 he moved to Indiana University where he was part of large-scale technical assistance programs to Thailand and the Philippines. All of these experiences, combined with his background in China, served to inform the development of his model "prismatic society." In Riggs's words: "There were two basic patterns for public administration, the first had evolved in traditional empires and kingdoms where pre-industrial social and economic conditions prevailed, and the second was a product of modernity following the industrial revolution and the emergence of the post-Westphalian state system.... I rejected the escalator model of the new modernization literature ... in which 'traditional' societies were expected to respond to the fresh breezes of 'modernity' by embracing changes that would, sooner or later, bring them into the new world of opportunity.... It stuck me that most societies would adhere tenaciously to many of their most valued ancient traditions and cultural norms while simultaneously importing and accepting a façade of practices and patterns that would, hopefully, enable them to maintain their distinctive cultures while benefiting from the autonomy and material goods offered by the outside world. Instead, curious amalgams would be formed in which agraria and industria would combine in unstable mixtures. In the prism of my imagination, the white light of undifferentiated social systems would mingle with the rainbow hues of highly differentiated social structures as found today in every industrialized society."

Bureaucracies are, Riggs argues, especially important in prismatic societies. As he points out: "American theories of public administration are predicated on the assumption that public officials are always under the ultimate control of a political institution based on notions of popular sovereignty.... My experience told me, however, that although copies of western political institutions might have been established ... they might be so weak that they could not govern effectively.... [I]t struck me as important to study how bureaucrats could and would shape public policy when they were, in effect, the ruling class." He invented the term "bureaucratic polity" and used it to describe countries with strong military bureaucracies such as China, Thailand, and Korea.

Although two generations have been schooled in the wisdom of Riggsian "prismatic society," we tend to succumb to pressures to export wholesale our public administration and democratic government ideas to non-western countries. Riggs would counsel care and caution: "The main lesson I learned in Korea was simply a reinforced version of my father's experience: Until one understands the dynamics of change in any society and takes them into account, one cannot expect to succeed in efforts to import rules and practices based on the experiences of other countries. At least, be prepared to find that these imported notions are counter-productive, leading to unexpected and undesired consequences."

Americans involved in Iraq and elsewhere would benefit from a careful reading of the work of Fred Riggs.

Since his formulation of "prismatic society," Riggs has moved on to other subjects including contrasting presidential and parliamentary constitutional systems (he argues that presidential systems are inherently less stable in prismatic societies), ethnicity, and globalization in the context of modern electronic technology. He remains active in comparative administration groups and is a relentless e-mail correspondent (fredr@hawaii.edu). He lives in Honolulu, retired from a distinguished teaching and research career at the University of Hawaii.

Lynton Keith Caldwell: The Man Who Invented Environmental Policy

Arguably the most important article ever printed in *Public Administration Review* (*PAR*) appeared in the September 1963 issue. In "Environment: A New Focus for Public Policy," Lynton Keith Caldwell laid out the framework for what was to become American environmental policy. Forty years later we see a global environmental movement—the so-called greens—as well as an established field of study and body of literature. It was Keith Caldwell, a leading public administration scholar, who, as much as anyone else, invented both a field of public policy and a global movement. I am happy to report that at age 91 Keith is among us still, talking and writing about environmental policy.

Caldwell's beginnings were an unlikely predicate to his emergence as a leading environmentalist. A son of the Midwest, he was born in 1913 in Montezuma, Iowa, where he was raised. Admitted to the University of Chicago, he majored in political science and there studied with several of the great early scholars in public administration including Leonard White, who wrote the first text in the field, Marshall Dimock, Wallace Sayre, Herman Finer, Charles Merriam, and Morton Grodzins. After earning an MA from Harvard he returned to Chicago for doctoral study and began teaching at the Gary and South Bend campuses of Indiana University. When he finished his doctorate, the University of Chicago Press decided to publish his dissertation and a wise decision it was. *The Administrative Theories of Hamilton and Jefferson* (1944) has been reprinted twice (1966 and 1986) and, along with Leonard White's books, it is the standard work on the subject. He published *PAR* articles in 1943 and 1944 on Jefferson and Hamilton, but when they are compared with his heavily referenced 1963 environmental policy article, these articles are obscure.

Two Chicago area environmental issues interested him at the time—political battles over the Calumet Marshes and the Indiana Dunes—but they were not at the center of his intellectual pursuits.

After the Second World War, Caldwell taught at the joint Maxwell School-NYU graduate program in Albany, New York. While he was in New York he followed the politics of the Hudson River basin, politics that eventually resulted in a large and successful river clean up. He also was active in the Nature Conservancy, but this activity was still primarily an avocation. The Caldwells then bounced around for a few years, spending time in Turkey, the Philippines, Berkeley and elsewhere. Finally, in the mid-1950s he took a position in political science on the main campus of Indiana University, and the family settled in Bloomington. By that time the Teddy Roosevelt era conservation movement was over and the preservation movement was on the wane. During the 1960s domestic American politics and policy had primarily to do with urbanization and attendant issues of planning, housing, schooling, transportation, public safety and race. In this era of growth, Caldwell was one of the few who saw the environmental consequences.

In his prescient 1963 *PAR* article Caldwell pointed out that there was "no clear doctrine of public responsibility for human environment as such. It therefore follows that concern for the environment is the business of almost no one in our public life." Now, not only is there a U.S. Environmental Protection Agency, many states and even some cities have such departments.

In 1963 he wrote that "the public decision-maker—legislative, administrative, or judicial—must deal with environmental questions without the help of a general body of environmental policy to which he might turn for authoritative guidance." Now there is the National Environmental Policy Act of 1969 (NEPA of 1969), on which Caldwell served as one of the principal drafters. Additionally there are now many other national, state, and local environmental laws.

In 1963 he wrote of the importance of "weighing environmental-affecting decisions on the basis of costs and benefits." Now every significant proposed change to the environment requires the preparation of an environmental impact statement, a concept he had built into the NEPA of 1969.

In 1963 Caldwell challenged segmented thinking and used the logic of ecology to develop out a more holistic approach to environmental matters. "American policies affecting the environment have been essentially segmental—largely because most of us, in government and out, taking the environment for granted, have dealt with its various elements without regard to their interrelated totality. In our pioneer traditions, we have been too busy cutting trees to think about the consequences to the environmental forest."

Leaving Hamilton and Jefferson behind, Caldwell dedicated himself to the development of environmental policy. In the early 1970s one of his colleagues, the public administration scholar John Ryan, was appointed president of Indiana University. Ryan was determined to build a top quality public administration program and saw in Caldwell's work the genesis of what became the School of Public and Environmental Affairs, today the leading center for environmental policy in the United States.

Caldwell has written over 200 articles and 12 books on environmental policy during the next 35 years, establishing himself as one of the intellectual fathers both of environmental policy and of the environmental movement. Along the way he received the Mosher, Burchfield, Dimock, and Gaus awards and served as a guest scholar at the Woodrow Wilson International Center. He has served on numerous boards and commissions, including the National Research Council and the Board of Governors of the Nature Conservancy. At home he recently received the Indiana University Distinguished Service Award.

In my own opinion his finest work is an article in *Politics and the Life Sciences* titled "Is Humanity Destined to Self-Destruct?" Here he writes: "Having abandoned reciprocity with the natural world in pursuit of command over it, modern civilization has broken an ancient covenant with nature.... Although humans have created the artificial environments called 'civilizations,' their survival is contingent upon living within the natural system from which they evolved. A critical challenge to humanity is to learn how to live in this natural-artificial hybrid environment which it is undertaking to manage.... Yet humans must accommodate to those forces of nature which cannot be managed beyond managing ourselves. Those who formulate policy should recognize that if humans pit themselves against the fundamental dynamics of cosmic nature, they are certain to lose."

One should not assume from the tone of despair in these words that Caldwell has no answers, because he does. Here are his suggestions for "what must be done to move from a course that possibly threatens global destruction to one of global sustainability.... The first is an analysis and evaluation of major social-environmental trends.... The second line of action, more difficult, is the universalizing of an ethic of environmental stewardship and sustainability.... The third line of action ... is persuasion through communication.... A fourth line of action is the selection and nurturing of democratic leaders able to communicate environmental imperatives."

In public administration Lynton Keith Caldwell provides an extraordinary example of the importance of ideas and the power of intellectual leadership.

Book Two
Leadership in Public Administration

Getting Leadership Straight

The former Secretary of the Navy, Richard Danzig, in a recent James Webb Lecture at the National Academy of Public Administration gave the most informed and thoughtful speech on public sector leadership and transformation I have heard in years. Here are a few highlights in Danzig's own words.

"Where do our ideas about leadership come from?

"They are derived from the business community ... people like Henry Ford or Edward Land and the Polaroid Camera or Steve Jobs or Bill Gates, people who had some notion about what they were going to do, the creators of FedEx and Wal-Mart, built from a different vision about organization.... The literature on these subjects is not built from government service; it is built from the world of business.... This model is what Jung would have called a "universal archetype." It is a Moses-like notion. Preach a new vision. Go up on the mountain and see it. Then lead the chosen people through 40 years in the wilderness to the Promised Land.

"Does this concept of leadership and transformation work in government?

"I think it's wrong. I think it's misleading. I think in many situations it's dangerous. Why?

"First of all it's remarkably arrogant. It's okay for Moses—he had access to God. But, if you look at all of our visions they are not so divinely inspired. Many such visions are, in fact, fundamentally wrong.... [In business] nine out of ten organizations fail. [As a public official] I've got a fundamental problem if I bet the organization on some monotonic conception of the future, because I can't play the odds.... I can't let nine navies fail, while the tenth succeeds, because we don't have ten navies.

"Second, you'll notice that it took Moses 40 years.... The average government appointee will serve for two years.

"Third, who was it Moses brought out of the Promised Land? His chosen people, not the Egyptians. As secretary of the Navy I've got to stay and persuade the Egyptians to do something different.

"What would be a better approach for the public sector?

"My view is that there is something better than the Moses example. It's a much more mundane, yet provocative model: the monkey who has his eyes covered, the monkey who has his ears covered, and the monkey who has his mouth covered.... We need to unstop our ears and listen. We need to look very closely. Then, we need to speak to the organization.

"[A] new appointee must listen to what the organization is telling him about what it cares about and what it values.... Some of the most interesting and important things the organization says about itself it says in the form of its clichés: 'People are our most important asset.' 'We are a team.' 'We live in a technological age." These propositions ... are right, they were here long before I arrived, they are universally shared, and everybody agrees on them.

"It was said of the philosopher Bronson Alcott that 'he soared into the infinite and fathomed the unfathomable, but never paid cash.' In our organizations we soar into the infinite and fathom the unfathomable in these great propositions, but we don't pay cash. We don't [invest the resources necessary to] translate them into the day-to-day life of the organization.... These banal clichés carry the seeds of revolution, the seeds of a dramatically different organization.... But, to get there you have to hear first what the organization is saying, look hard at those propositions and see where they lead you, and follow their logic relentlessly ... and then speak to them ... [by] figuring out how to pay cash.... Personnel systems change.... Different kinds of people get promoted.... [You invest in] a single uniform information system. [These investments] follow from premises that everybody accepts, and from premises that people have sworn they're going to live by. It leads, I think, to a quite different kind of result.

"Persuading any group of people is to start where they are, not where you are. It's to listen first to what they care about and what they're thinking and what they're organizing around and then if you want to move them ... show them how that logic leads elsewhere than they may have thought it led. That seems to me to be a fundamental technique in government that is under-represented and underutilized.

"None of us is Moses.... [We should not] recreate the business model, creating new companies while leaving the old to die. The effects on government would be disastrous. [When compared with even the best of businesses] we have a vastly harder job, a bigger challenge, and one that requires us to convert the Egyptians.

"It is intrinsically not at all something that is borne of the genius of a leader. Virtually none of the organization's ideas are my own. The organization is generating them, seeing clearly the themes we care about. No one is as smart as everyone. [Together we] see the unity of effort because the unity of effort begins in things we all believe in, not in some outsider preaching some radical new proposition.

"[T]here's a new world of opportunity nascent in all our organizations, and my suggestion to you is we don't get there by preaching our vision; we get there by opening our eyes to what's going on around us. There are great possibilities ... because we are talking about people who are committed to begin with and who have visions of their own."

Public Administration and Quiet Leadership

Much of what is written about leadership is based on the study of heroic, swashbuckling, culture transforming, business executives—a literature ill-suited to the study or practice of public administration. There is, however, an exception: the one book on leadership that should be on every public administrator's bookshelf: *Leading Quietly: An Unorthodox Guide to Doing the Right Thing* by Joseph L. Badarocco, Jr.

Because quiet leaders are in it for the long haul they tend to be realists about themselves, about their organizations, and about the contingent nature of the environment in which they work. Quiet leaders tend to move carefully, step-by-step, in a generally agreed-upon direction. They recognize the age-old wisdom of effective planning—that no war plan survives the first battle. Good planning is a deeply contingent process. Plans always change depending on shifting resources, technologies, dangers and opportunities. Quiet leaders are also realistic about their power—acutely aware of the limits and subtleties of power, even for leaders with impressive titles. In short, quiet leaders don't kid themselves.

Conventional stories of great leadership, Mother Teresa, for example, portray the leader as a person of pure motives, high aims, and noble causes. Not so. Quiet leaders understand and even learn to trust mixed motives. Altruism, courage, self-sacrifice, and dedication to great causes are splendid motives; but so too are ambition, recognition, and personal success, not to mention survival. In decision circumstances involving complex motives (are there any other kind?) Badarocco indicates that the effective leader:

- has a bias for action and does not get bogged down in the morass of motives
- does not disqualify him or herself because of mixed motives
- learns to trust competing motives and to recognize the trade-offs involved
- understands that organizational effectiveness and personal success are usually compatible outcomes.

Time is on the side of the quiet leader. Effective leaders avoid, whenever possible, rushing forward with the answer. Instead they buy time, appoint committees, do studies, and wait until turbulent waters calm and a plausible course of action is evident. Quick fixes are just that. Quiet leaders will practice tactical stalling until a strategic direction is more-or-less clear, then move the organization step-by-step in that direction. While quiet leaders have a bias for action, they recognize that time is almost always their friend.

Quiet leaders think carefully about how they spend and invest their organizational capital. Because leadership always involves risk, the prudent assessment of risk is essential to any important decision. Quiet leaders will tackle tough situations but will not foolishly risk either the organization's capabilities or all of their own good will. In the literature, leaders are exhorted to "do the right thing." That is too simple because it calls for courage but says nothing about cost and risk.

The ordinary view of leadership has a generic, disembodied quality to it—as if to suggest that great leaders are able to lead effectively in any setting. Although most of us know this to be nonsense, it is nevertheless the formulaic description of leadership. Badarocco calls such a view of leadership what it is—nonsense—and argues correctly that there can be no great leadership, quiet or otherwise, without a deep substantive knowledge of the technological and bureaucratic characteristics of the specific setting in which leadership is expected. Context matters and the governmental context matters greatly, as any public administrator knows. The senior position in a government agency is no place for neophytes to get on-the-job leadership training. Quiet leaders, as Badarocco puts it, drill down to levels of complexity so they know what they are doing. Organizational matters, particularly in government, are never simple and seldom yield to simple answers.

Public administrators work in the world of constitutions, laws, appropriations, regulations, and rules. The common formula in the business literature is that responsible leaders selectively break the rules. Indeed there is a good bit of evidence that too many business executives have believed the nonsense about the efficacy of breaking the rules. Now they will need to tell it to the judge. Taking rules seriously is the safe, smart and responsible thing to do in most public administration cases. When the rules get in the way of acting responsibly or ethically, quiet leaders will patiently find the pathway between the rules.

In the end, what do quiet leaders do? They compromise. Compromise is, of course, not in the vocabulary of those who subscribe to the heroic leader thesis. But, to quiet leaders, compromises are challenges to their imagination and ingenuity and occasions for hard, serious work. They believe that crafting a compromise is often a valuable way to learn and exercise practical wisdom. In their minds, the best compromises have little to do with splitting the difference or sacrificing important values to pragmatic considerations. Instead, they are powerful ways of defending and expressing important values in enduring practical ways. Crafting responsible, workable compromises is not just something that quiet leaders do. It defines who they are.

Public Administration as Gardening

It is one thing to know public administration, but it is quite another to understand it. Over the past few years a group of thoughtful people have developed a particularly wise and useful way to understand and think about public administration—gardening. Understandings of public administration as gardening appear to trace to a short paragraph in a little out-of-print book edited by Peter Szanton. At the end of a very good study of patterns of federal government reorganization, he wrote: "So reorganization had best be viewed as a branch of gardening rather than of architecture or engineering. As in gardening, the possibilities are limited by soil and climate, and accomplishment is slow. Like gardening, reorganization is not an act but a process, a continuing job. And like gardening, reorganization is work whose benefits may largely accrue to one's successors." This insight has been picked up and developed by the so-called institutionalists, led by James March and Johan Olsen. Based on extensive reviews of the empirical literature their synthesis of public administration and gardening includes the following understandings.

Public administration as gardening begins with the wisdom of John Gaus. He advised us to build, quite literally, from the ground up; from the elements of a place—soils, climate, location, and people. It is within this setting that their instruments and practices of public housekeeping should be studied so that they may better understand what they are doing, and appraise reasonably how they are doing it.

Gardening, as an understanding of public administration, following Gaus, makes demands upon our powers to observe, upon a sensitive awareness of changes and maladjustment and upon our willingness to face the political—that is, the public housekeeping—basis of administration. Gardening, like the powers of observation and awareness in public administration, requires time, patience, and experience. Seasons matter because planning done in the winter is often more important than hard work in the spring and summer. Experienced public administrators know seasons—the budget cycle, the legislative cycle, the unique rhythms, patterns and routines of each organization. Our best gardeners know when to prune, to plan, to plant, and to cultivate.

Gardeners work with available resources—soil, water, seeds, climate. And so it is with public administration. In our better practices, public administration gardeners are shrewd managers of these resources and among these resources none are more important than the plants—the people. A genuine caring for and knowledge of each plant and an understanding of each plant's potential marks the difference between the casual planter of seeds and the gardener. Being responsible for the whole garden, the gardener must also know how all plants and group of plants can be harmoniously related to make a beautiful garden. Plants need nourishment, water, sunshine, and encouragement. And the good gardener knows the limits of resources and the capacities of each plant and works carefully within those limits. So it is with public administration.

Changes in the garden, as in public organizations, tend to be incremental. Present circumstances, the condition of the garden, in the words of Johan Olsen, are usually the result of long historical processes, involving conflicts, victories, defeats and compromises, as well as processes of interpretation, learning, and habituation. It is difficult to subject institutional evolution to tight control and history becomes a meander. Working with what they have inherited, gardeners understand that change is experimental, step-by-step, and subject to the power of uncontrollable external forces. Nevertheless, patient gardeners know that a five percent annual change in the garden, compounded annually, will, in a few years, make a mighty change in the garden. It is not unusual, in the rhythms of gardening, for a particular plan or experiment to fail the first or second season. But persistence pays, in the words of March and Olsen: "Sometimes short-run failures turn into long-run successes,

41

as old plans are reactivated under new and more favorable circumstances."

The modern literature of administration (particularly business administration) is saturated with images of powerful, heroic leaders—risk-takers, entrepreneurs, agents of change. Understanding institutional values and traditions is not especially important because it is assumed that those values and traditions need to be changed. In such models of administration it is all about the gardener. Is it any wonder that the risks and changes such heroic gardeners attempt usually fail? To understand public administration as gardening is to know that it is all about the garden, not the gardener. In the long run, the patient public administration gardener will, working with the resources at hand, plan, adapt, guide, and nurture processes of genuine and lasting institutional change. This spring the gardens of public administration are especially in need of our best gardeners.

Book Three
Real Public Administration Leaders

David O. Cooke: Mayor of the Pentagon

What official administered the oath of office to Secretary of Defense Donald Rumsfeld on the night of the first inauguration of President George W. Bush? The answer to this bit of trivia tells a particularly compelling story about the best of public administration and about the importance of the permanent federal service.

His name is David O. Cooke, but everyone called him "Doc." To give you an idea of Doc Cooke's standing in the Department of Defense (DoD), consider this: Not only did he administer the oath of office to Secretary Rumsfeld, he also administered the oath to Rumsfeld twenty-five years earlier, during the Ford Administration! During his career, Doc Cooke served fourteen different secretaries of Defense.

Consider this pedigree. After a BS from what is now the State University of New York at Buffalo, an MS from the State University of New York at Albany, and an LL.B from George Washington University, Cooke went on active duty in the U.S. Navy in 1951. While in the Navy he was on the faculty of the School of Naval Justice, later a staff member of the Judge Advocate General (JAG), and then, during the Eisenhower administration in 1958, he was made a member of Secretary of Defense McElroy's task force on DoD reorganization. His work on that task force was so effective that, in 1961 he was one of the initial staff appointed to the newly established Office of Organization and Management Planning, to implement the recommendations of the task force. Then, in 1964 he took over as director of that office. In 1967 he left active duty in the Navy and moved to the civilian side of the Pentagon. From 1969 to 1988 he served as deputy assistant secretary for administration, the top civilian management position in the Pentagon. In 1988 that position was given greater autonomy and he became the director of administration and management for the Department of Defense.

To give an example of Doc Cooke's standing in the Pentagon, consider this little story told by James B. King, former director of the U.S. Office of Personnel Management.

A few years ago a new secretary of defense arrived at the Pentagon for his first day on the job and was stopped at the door by a security guard.

"Where is your ID?" the guard asked.

"I'm sorry," the new secretary said. "But they haven't issued me one yet."

"Then you can't come in, pal," the guard said.

"You don't understand," the newcomer said. "I'm the new secretary of defense."

The guard said, "Mister, I don't care if you're Doc Cooke—nobody gets in without an ID."

At about the time of the transition between the Clinton and Bush administrations, outgoing Secretary of Defense William Cohen held an "end of the administration" party. At that party, in addition to Cohen, were the new secretary, Donald Rumsfeld, the vice president elect and former secretary of defense, Dick Cheney, the outgoing secretary of the navy, Richard Danzig, and a host of incoming and outgoing DoD political appointees. Whom were they there to honor? Doc Cooke, the "Mayor of the Pentagon," that's whom! In a toast, Secretary Cohen said this of Doc Cooke: "You embody all the values and virtues that America could hope for in a public servant—unwavering honor, unquestioned integrity, and an unequaled commitment to the nation. And, you are a person who always gets the job done."

Timothy B. Clark, the editor and publisher of *Government Executive* magazine, attributes Doc Cooke's effectiveness to a combination of unquestioned moral authority and unwavering support for the men and women of the armed forces. Cooke's moral authority is rooted in the primary public administration values of politically neutral management, fair and evenhanded leadership, informed competence, and responsiveness to democratically elected leaders. As is always the case in military affairs, his moral authority is also based on an abiding loyalty to and understanding of the rank and file, lessons learned in the Navy and never forgotten. His belief in and understanding of the larger purposes of national defense and his enthusiastic pursuit of those purposes informs Cooke's moral authority. Finally, his authority is based on a positive view of human capacity and an infectious optimism about the possibilities of organizational betterment.

There was, in the early stages of the Clinton administration, a strong commitment to the so-called reinventing government concept, and Vice President Gore took up the assignment of leading the implementation of that concept through the National Performance Review (NPR). In the midst of the many DoD skeptics and cynics who had seen reforms and reorganizations come and go, Doc Cooke took another view. He knew the logical flaws in the reinventing paradigm, but with his usual enthusiasm and optimism he took the position that the NPR was a good way to make improvements in Pentagon and DoD effectiveness. Under Doc Cooke's guidance, over the next several years, in the face of significant downsizing, DoD was able to demonstrate increased mission readiness, and better housing, education, and health care for the rank and file, while saving money. This seems a wonderful example of reasoned bureaucratic responsiveness to democratically elected officials while at the same time protecting the core purpose of national defense.

It is one thing to describe the importance of organizational continuity and institutional memory in government. It is another thing to see it in action. In the midst of Washington's political whirl, Doc Cooke's career was a perfect illustration of why continuity and institutional memory are critical. After a generation of bureaucracy bashing, anti-government rhetoric and downsizing, almost all studies indicate that the permanent federal service is in serious trouble. Prior to September 11, 2001, most young people had little interest in direct government service. The single most important issue in national security rests on attracting and retaining sufficient numbers of qualified people to serve in government. Doc Cooke grew up in an era of grand and noble purposes and a positive government bent on carrying out those purposes. Over the last

30 years, and until recently, our collective purposes have been less grand and noble and big government seemed out of place. The need to find young Doc Cookes and attract them to public service seemed unimportant. Perhaps recent events will start the processes of change.

John Gilbert Winant and British–American Relations in a Time of Crisis

John Gilbert Winant was the U.S. Ambassador to Great Britain throughout the Second World War. Before that, Gil, as he was known, served in both the New Hampshire House and Senate and was then elected governor, the youngest in the United States at the time. He was twice more elected governor. He helped draft the Social Security Act of 1935 and, after its passage, was asked by President Franklin Delano Roosevelt to serve as the Republican representative on the first Social Security board. In the 1936 presidential campaign, the Republican challenger, Alf Landon, repudiated the Social Security Act. Gil believed in the act so strongly that he resigned his position on the board and came out for Roosevelt to be reelected, not an easy step for a New Hampshire Republican.

By the late 1930s Nazi Germany and the Axis had conquered Europe, driven the English off the Continent at Dunkirk and were poised 20 miles from Dover. Nightly raids were bombing English towns and cities to rubble. It seemed just a matter of time before the Germans invaded across the English Channel. The U.S. Ambassador to Great Britain at the time, Joseph P. Kennedy, described as "electric, articulate, breezy, direct, and indiscreet," was strongly opposed to American involvement in the European war. He insisted that "England was gone. Not only had German bombs paralyzed industry and communication lines, Britain was bankrupt, unable to meet commitments to the United States." Finally, in late 1940, Kennedy resigned to return home to "help the President keep the U.S. out of war." He found the Congress in a heated debate over the extent to which the U.S. should cooperate with and aid Great Britain.

As England held the line against Germany alone, President Roosevelt appointed John Gilbert Winant to be the United States Ambassador to the Court of St. James. Winant was tall, awkward, soft spoken—the un-Kennedy. Each morning after the bombing raids he and his staff walked the streets helping in any way they could. For the next seven years Winant served as the primary conduit between President Roosevelt and Prime Minister Winston Churchill. More important, he was at Churchill's side at every step in the recovery of Great Britain, preparations for the invasion of France, and eventual victory in the European theater in the Second World War. Upon his return to the United States, the *London Daily Express* wrote: "Second only to Mr. Roosevelt, Mr. Winant has seemed to us the personification of the finest part of America's character. We shall miss that tall, thoughtful, awkward seeming man." King George awarded him the honorary British Order of Merit, and the Queen said to him: "You deserve it more than anyone."

Winant wrote this about relations between Britain and America during England's darkest hour: "You could not live in London in those early years and not realize how narrow was the margin of survival. It would have taken so few mistakes to bring about defeat, the miracle was how few were made and how unimportant in retrospect they were, although in war none is ever without importance, since all decisions touch life and death. It has seemed to me that many people do not understand the urgency of those days. Nor do I think it is sufficiently appreciated how much the British gave us in return for what we gave them, not only in loyalty and friendship, but in practical contributions."

Fifty years later, friends and family have endowed the John Gilbert Winant Visiting Professorship in American Government at Oxford to recognize his distinguished public service and to mark the enduring friendship of our two nations. One of the stipulations of the endowment is that the professorship be held by an American.

At the risk of oversimplification, this brief review of British-American relations in a time of war, and the role of public servants like John G. Winant, can help us answer a particularly vexing question.

How, with most of Europe in opposition, can one explain the steadfast support of the British government for the preemptive American war against Iraq? The war is unpopular with the majority of British people, and Prime Minister Tony Blair is in trouble. His government has been buffeted by cabinet resignations, the suicide of a leading civil servant, and a Parliamentary inquiry into whether the threat of weapons of mass destruction in Iraq had been, to use the British phrase, sexed-up. Although the United States and Great Britain, and the so-called coalition, now occupy Iraq, winning the peace will take much longer than winning the war, even the war on terrorism. The British government and Tony Blair are standing with the United States for reasons that can only be understood by history.

Today most British people have no direct memory of the blitz or of how close their country came to defeat, but every school kid knows the stories of the bombs, the destruction, and the death. And they all know that it was the United States who came to the aid of England in their darkest hour. Because of this the televised destruction of the World Trade Center and the damage to the Pentagon were images with special meaning to the British. One can agree or disagree with the Bush administration on the preemptive war against Iraq, and one can agree or disagree that the war was in part justified on the basis of claims of weapons of mass destruction in Iraq. These debates are likely to dominate both American and British politics for the upcoming months and years. Even in the context of these debates and in the face of strong political opposition, one must agree that the support of the Blair administration for the war in Iraq is a contemporary manifestation of the historical friendship between Great Britain and the United States. The United States, at great sacrifice of life and treasure, stood by the British fifty years ago, when they were most in need. And now, right or wrong, the British are standing by the United States in its war on terrorism. Only time will tell whether they are on the right course or on a fool's errand.

Honor in the Public Life

On September 11, 2001, in a swift and horrible moment, much about contemporary public administration changed. Now, the contours of a changed public administration are coming into focus.

One of the most useful ways to describe perceptions of and attitudes toward both government and public administration in the 1980s and 1990s was the word "disconnect." Citizens were disconnected and alienated from their public institutions and attitudes toward both elected officials and the public service were negative. Although we proclaimed ourselves to practice democratic self-government, governmental institutions were thought to be something separate—those people in Washington, or Sacramento, or city hall. In the abundance of a good economy and the security of our power, we were disconnected from each other and from our institutions.

There was little honor in the public life. Despite exhortations calling us to a greater concern for one another and for our institutions, it took the terrible events of September 11th to connect us together again.

Nameless and faceless public servants, once so easy to ridicule, now have names and faces. Brady Howell, age 26, a recent Maxwell MPA, serves as a Presidential Management Internship in the Pentagon. George Howard, age 45, is a New York Port Authority police officer. Daniel Becthel, age 40, is a captain in the New York City Fire Department. Edward Earhart, age 26, of Salt Lick, Kentucky, is an aerographer's mate first class in the U.S. Navy, assigned to the Pentagon. The list goes on and on.

All the public servants who died are heroes. And the New York City police, fire, and emergency services personnel and all of those from other departments working in the recovery are also our heroes. Their names and faces and their remarkable service clarify this point—the public service is no longer them, the public service is us. Once again there is honor in the public life.

When things go wrong, badly wrong, we turn as if by instinct to our cities, our states and our nation. At noon on Friday, September 14th,

2001 huge crowds gathered on the grounds of almost all of the state capitols and at hundreds of city halls and other public places to reconnect; to sing and pray together; and to listen to mayors, governors, fire and police chiefs, and other public officials. The unique connection between the people and their governments that we call democratic self-government was on full display, not just with the federal government but with state and local governments as well. At these meetings and in many other places there is a return to civility and the high citizenship characterized by individual sacrifice and service to others.

Together, both as citizens and as public administrators, we face the challenges of terrorism. Terrorism, unlike conventional enemies, is the work of the stateless—global networks able to all but disregard borders and state sovereignty. Terrorism, like environmental pollution, nuclear proliferation, and organized crime, has little respect for borders. Combating such enemies will require the United States to be both sovereign and carefully networked. We are in a state of high interdependence, and in such a state our networks are as important as our sovereignty. The diminished capacity of borders to contain problems calls for highly developed forms of interjurisdictional cooperation and coordination. While some of this cooperation and coordination is political, much of it is administrative. Combating global terrorism will only happen if like-minded and dedicated public service professionals work together in a state of high cooperation and coordination. While public servants are employed by particular jurisdictions (a few work for regional or global organizations), we all understand interdependence. The skilled practice of multijurisdictional administrative coalition building and maintenance is part of the job description of the 21st century public administrator. Combating global terrorism will require a fixed eye on the long-run, great administrative creativity, and sacrifice—all qualities of the best in public administration. Once the policies are established, combating terrorism will require the resources necessary to do the job and the latitude to let the public service do that job.

In the present arid landscape of diminished institutions, management fads, policy gimmicks, and leadership rhetoric, we must return to our core values and practices. We must be as prepared as we are able for much more serious problems than the field has faced in the past 30 years, for such serious problems will surely come.

But with those problems has come a possible reconnection between the people and their governmental institutions, a sharply increased respect for public servants and public service, and a renewed sense of collective determination and sacrifice. When faced with daunting questions and big challenges the American people have turned to their political institutions for answers and for effective responses to those challenges. After setting the course of action, our political leaders have in turn called on the American public service, at all levels of government, to implement that course of action. As in the past, this call will be honored with determination, vigor, and patriotism. That is because there is, after all, honor in the public life.

William Armstrong: Public Service Leadership

Consider the civil service career of William Armstrong. Unlike those from the aristocracy of privilege who still tend to reach the top of the British senior civil service, Armstrong was anything but high born. His working class parents were officers in the Salvation Army, and he grew up in an austere atmosphere of no radio, cinema, or alcohol. They moved often, the children attending schools in the slum districts in which their parents worked. William, lacking musical talent, carried the banner at Salvation Army street meetings and revivals. Against strong competition from those with privileged backgrounds, he won admission and a scholarship to the University of Oxford. There he read the classics and took a coveted first. He then took the civil service entrance examinations and finished fifth in the competition for the higher civil service. His first assignment was to the British Board of Education where he became the only person in the administrative grades who had actually been through the system of education they were administering.

It was the late 1930s and war was looming. Armstrong was made secretary to a committee chaired by the permanent secretary dealing with the subject of the evacuation of children in wartime. In the daily meetings of that committee his razor sharp mind, communication skills, and organizational capacity brought him to the attention of persons in power. This process and variants on it became the template for a remarkable series of rapid promotions through the ranks. Most important was an appointment as private secretary to the Secretary of the War Cabinet. He virtually lived in the war ministry and was, therefore, close to or among most of the senior officials of British government. At the end of WW II in Europe, he represented Britain in the organization of the Potsdam peace conference. There is a photograph showing Atlee, Bevin, Stalin, Truman, and Molotov standing together, with William Armstrong sitting at a table in the background. He was 30 years old.

In the early 1950s he served as principal private secretary to three successive Chancellors of the Exchequer, two from Labor (Cripps and Gaitskell) and one from the Conservatives (Butler). He seemed to instinctively understand "the nature of the political animal" and to know how to adapt to it. He wrote most of five annual Budget speeches and came to be regarded as the government's leading expert on economic and financial issues. In the early 1960s he was appointed as a joint permanent secretary for economic and financial policy, leapfrogging several others to the third highest position in the British civil service. In late 1962 Armstrong was appointed by Prime Minister Harold Macmillan to the top position, permanent secretary in the Treasury. At age 46 he was now one of the "Treasury knights," and was the youngest Treasury permanent secretary in memory. He was the last of the classicists to head Treasury—subsequent permanent secretaries all having read (majored in) economics in college. Through reading and experience he had made himself economically literate.

Dissatisfied with what he believed to be a slow moving, cumbersome, and cautious Treasury, Macmillan was determined to shake things up. Shortly after Armstrong's appointment, the political leadership of the Treasury, the Chancellor of the Exchequer, was sacked along with one-third of the Cabinet. This was followed by a radical reorganization of the

Treasury, mostly engineered by Armstrong. The overall management of the civil service was removed from Treasury and made essentially a separate department. In his six years at Treasury he was among the most powerful British public officials. How does a civil servant reconcile objectivity and neutrality on one hand and the exercise of power on the other? Here are his words: "The biggest and most pervasive influence is in setting the framework within which the questions of policy are raised. We, while I was in the Treasury, had a framework of the economy [which was] basically neo-Keynesian. We set the questions which we asked the ministers to decide arising out of that framework and it would have been enormously difficult for any minister to change the framework, so to that extent we had great power."

In 1968, Armstrong moved over to become the first permanent secretary of the newly formed Civil Service Department. He was hailed as the "new broom" reformer who would bring modernization to the bureaucracy. He cultivated a higher profile, appearing on radio and television interview shows and even holding press conferences. He disagreed with the anonymity and facelessness of the civil service. Although these activities are now practiced by many permanent secretaries, at the time it was quite out of senior civil service character.

In the early 1970s political leadership had shifted to the Tory, Edward Heath. Then, as Kevin Theakston puts it, "William Armstrong's role in the Heath government extended far beyond his formal responsibilities as Head of the Civil Service—in some ways beyond what was strictly proper for any civil servant," Heath preferred to surround himself with senior civil servants, the mandarins, rather than Cabinet ministers, political friends or party advisors. To Heath, Armstrong became the indispensable man, the informal "deputy prime minister" as Armstrong came to be derisively described in the press. He took to sitting alongside the prime minister at press conferences and making political statements at meetings. In 1974, Heath was defeated by Labor and Harold Wilson stepped in as prime minister. Armstrong, by then overidentified with Heath, would leave the civil service and moved to the Midland Bank as Chair.

The Armstrong story tells us much about British public administration. It illustrates the resilience of British class privilege in the senior civil service, but it also shows that competence and merit matter. Armstrong, a man of formidable intellectual ability, was the archetypical detached, analytical, imperturbable, and loyal senior civil servant. He served the elected officials of both parties equally well and worked effectively with a very wide range of personality types and ideologies. He was relentlessly fair and dedicated to equality and particularly a champion of fairness for women—often pointing out that his mother outranked his father in the Salvation Army. He saw the coming importance of management to the higher civil service and described modern permanent secretaries as "policy managers rather than policy advisors or policy originators."

The British senior civil service could be fairly described as a model of "administrative conservatorship," to use Larry D. Terry's term. The enduring institutional capabilities of government are important to them and they see themselves as the guardians of those institutions. Although he was a reformer, William Armstrong engaged in reform with an eye toward institutional integrity.

Top civil servants are leaders but are themselves on a political lead, a lead that can be quickly shortened. Armstrong once said that top civil servants must "operate on the edge of politics without being political." During most of his brilliant career William Armstrong seemed to instinctively know where that line was and just as instinctively kept himself on the civil service side. But, near the end of his career, his nose for power and his need to be at the center of things caused him to cross that line and go political and, as one observer put it, betray his caste.

Jesse Fraser: A Radical Bureaucrats in the Stacks

There was a time when librarians had serious names—Marion, Ruth, Sybil, Belle. As a schoolboy the one I knew best was Jesse Fraser, the director and head librarian of the Twin Falls, ID, Public Library. In the library she was Miss Fraser, but outside the kids referred to her as Jesse. She called me young man, as she called the other schoolboys. This formality put me in my place, let me know I was in her house. I liked her, as did the other boys and girls, because she seemed to know everything and where to find everything. She hushed us when we were rowdy and sometimes even asked us to leave, but she never ratted to our parents. We sensed the pleasure it gave her to guide us to what we were looking for. We knew it was her job, but we knew it was more than her job. Miss Fraser, as we said those days, was "a stand up gal." She is gone, but the library she built is still a glorious place, larger now and all fancied up with computers and high tech.

Miss Fraser, it turns out, was an industrial strength bureaucrat and the operations of the local library were an early lesson in bureaucracy. Max Weber would have loved the Twin Falls Public Library. It had it all —hierarchy, division of labor, coordination, records to keep, sanctions for not returning books, a code of conduct, and a deep sense of responsibility and purpose. This library was not customer driven because Miss Fraser knew what library patrons needed, and she also knew that many patrons, particularly the kids, had no idea what they needed. There was no competitive outsourcing, no spreadsheets, no performance measures. Above all, there was no political intrusion or micromanagement. Miss Fraser stood up to those who would ban the books or magazines they did not like. You didn't mess with Miss Fraser. Although the word "radical" is hardly a word one would associate with a librarian, Miss Fraser was a radical bureaucrat with a bun.

It is pleasing to report that bureaucratic radicalism still flourishes in the stacks. It comes to me that Anne M. Turner, director of the Santa Cruz, CA, Public Library System has instructed her staff to daily shred the logs of the names of people who have used the Internet, written requests at the Reference Desk, or left other evidence of having been a library patron. When asked why this is being done, she gave a particularly un-librarian-like response: "The basic strategy now is to keep as little historical information as possible." This is because the Santa Cruz Library and other libraries around the country are protesting that part of the USA Patriot Act that allows agents of the Federal Bureau of Investigation (FBI) to review library and bookstore transactions including the records of those who borrow books or use the Internet. Many librarians believe this part of the Patriot Act infringes on Constitutional First Amendment freedom of speech protections. Turner said, "I am more terrified of having my First Amendment rights to information and free speech infringed than I am by the kinds of terrible acts that have come so far." But, because she is unwilling to break the law, the records are simply being shredded. Never underestimate the pluck and guile of a librarian.

Turner reports that the response of folks in Santa Cruz has been positive. The American Library Association reports that, so far, 225 of the 1,500 local public libraries in the United States indicate that they will practice a kind of bureaucratic passive resistance to that part of the law licensing federal agents to snoop into library records.

In addition to shredding, which does not break the law, the libraries of Santa Cruz posted this sign:

"Warning: Although the Santa Cruz Library makes every effort to protect your privacy, under the USA Patriot Act (Public Law 170.56) records of the books and other materials you borrow from this library may be obtained by federal agents. That law prohibits library workers from informing you if federal agents have obtained records about you. Questions about this policy should be directed to [former] Attorney General John Ashcroft, Department of Justice, Washington, DC 20530."

Who knows what affect this sign is having on library patrons, but it is a wonderfully subtle display of bureaucratic passive resistance. One might dismiss Turner and the folks at the Santa Cruz Public Library because it is, after all, in California, where such behavior might be expected. That would be a mistake. This is not about California; it is about librarians. Librarians are, in my experience, careful, thoughtful, deliberate and, dare I say, conservative. They are, however, passionate zealots on a mission to defend the freedom of information, wily and astute bureaucrats carefully protecting the institutional purposes of public libraries while, at the same time, protecting the liberties of their patrons.

It is a comfort to know that FBI agents are out there hunting for terrorists. It is also a comfort to know that librarians are doing what they can to protect our constitutional liberties. I have no doubt that professional librarians will report suspicious patrons who might be terrorists. But I also have no doubt that professional librarians will do all they can to protect the constitutional rights of patrons.

Here's the best to you, Miss Fraser, to you Ms. Turner, and to librarians everywhere. Promise me you will never change.

Simon David Freeman: The California Electricity Czar

The California energy crisis can be traced in large part to one of the big reform ideas of the last generation—deregulation. In the reform hegemony of the 1990s, markets and competition were god, government was the devil, and regulation the devil's tool. The California legislature, in the passion of this reform, deregulated electric utilities. In return the corporate electric utilities and many of their electric power suppliers made themselves semi-autonomous subdivisions of larger corporations and those corporations sucked the California wealth out of them and used it to pay stockholder dividends, high executive salaries and benefits and to buy and operate corporate jets. They also made this gamble: "If together we limit the supply of electric power, rate increases will be necessary."

I know. I know. It is fashionable to claim that if California had done it right and deregulated electricity properly then this reform would have worked. It is also fashionable to claim that those darned environmentalists were the problem. And, of course, we can always point to NIMBY. Let me suggest that these claims are both mostly wrong and entirely misleading.

Perhaps, like me, you have noticed that proponents of a particular change in public policy label their preferred change a "reform," thereby, we assume, investing their preferred policy with the allure of the better idea. In California in the mid-1990s deregulating electricity was the reform, the better idea. By having labeled their preferred public policy a reform, the utilities could describe those who oppose their reform the defenders of old ideas, reactionary fossils imbedded in the status quo. Centuries ago Aristotle described the techniques of political rhetoric and argued that the use of rhetorical techniques could powerfully move public policy. That is exactly what happened in California. There was virtually no policy analysis. There was virtually no data indicating that deregulating corporate electric utilities would result in competition and a genuine electricity market. Never mind. In the world of policymaking, winning rhetoric will always trump facts and policy analysis. Deregulation as a winning political slogan was everywhere evident in the 1990s. So, believing their own rhetoric the California legislature let the corporate electric utilities essentially draft a deregulation bill. Then they gambled that deregulation would work and they gambled that the corporate electricity utilities would be good citizens.

Perhaps, like me, you will also have noticed that when a reform doesn't work, the proponents of that reform claim that the reform was not implemented properly. The reform is good, they say, it is just those bumbling public administrators who cannot pull it off. Nothing is, of course, wrong with their reform. Let me suggest that the California electricity deregulation reform was wrongheaded to begin with. Reform proponents, still gallantly carrying on, argue that if the California State Legislature, when it approved electric deregulation, had allowed corporate utilities to set customer prices then their reform would have worked. They are right. It would have worked very well for the corporations, their stockholders, and their executives. It would, however, have worked very badly for electricity customers.

Did the environmentalists hold up the construction of new power generating facilities in California? No. In fact the Sierra Club formally approved several generating plant plans that the corporate utilities chose not to build in the hope of limiting the supply of electricity. Does NIMBY explain the failure to build electric capacity? Yes, to some extent, but it is a safe guess that, in the face of local opposition and in light of their interest in limiting supply, the utilities did not work especially hard to overcome NIMBY problems.

When such reforms fail there is always a cry for governmental action. That is the good news. Rather than deregulation, California is seriously considering regulation. Rather than privatization, California is govenmentalizing some aspects of the generation and provision of electricity, claiming that electricity is both a public and a private good and that it is now in the public interest to intervene. Finally, the City of Los Angeles did not embrace the electric utility reform and the people of Los Angeles are the better for it. That lesson is not lost on Californians.

Meet Simon David Freeman, the guy who pulled California out of its energy crisis.

First off, this guy is sooo un-California. He is 5 feet 7 inches tall, wears a tan cowboy hat indoors and out, and speaks with a Tennessee drawl. He has no tattoos and no earring, he drives a Plymouth, and he shows no evidence of cosmetic surgery. He is 75 years old, but even when he was young he did not suffer fools. Richard Ross of Sacramento says that Simon David Freeman "has no tolerance for pretense. It's not that he's a character; it's just that he's never allowed any varnish to be applied. He's like a great baseball bat—real wood. He doesn't need a consultant to tell him what to do." Phil Isenberg, former state assembly-men from Sacramento, says that Freeman "can be just terribly difficult to get along with. But, you forgive the momentary stuff for the strength of his character and the depth of his experience and the fact that he will be plain."

So, former Governor Gray Davis chose Simon David Freeman to be the California public power czar—the guy who would negotiate with the energy supply companies over the prices they charge; the guy who will strongly influence, if not determine, what the electric utilities can charge their customers; the guy who will try to get more electric generating capacity on-line as soon as possible. This would be a load for anyone, but a little 75-year-old cowboy-hat-wearing guy from Tennessee?

Who is this guy?

He was born in Chattanooga, the son of an immigrant Jewish umbrella repairman and a mother who worked in the family store. As a little boy he saw Franklin D. Roosevelt drive by in an open car. As a kid he experienced discrimination and recalls when New Testaments were handed out in his grade school. He earned engineering and law degrees from public universities and served in the Merchant Marines in World War II. In the 1950s he was part of sit-ins that forced a Knoxville diner to integrate. He worked as an energy advisor in both the Johnson and the Nixon White House and then as an energy advisor to the Senate Commerce Committee.

President Jimmy Carter appointed him to be the head of the Tennessee Valley Authority, the nation's largest publicly owned utility. For Freeman this was a dream come true. The TVA had brought electricity to much of the rural South and still rates just below high school football in the hearts and minds of Southerners. But when Freeman took over in the 1970s there was an energy crisis. Both public and investor owned utilities were at that time busy building nuclear power plants, and the TVA was no exception. Freeman was one of the first to realize that nuclear power was a financial bust. He says: "We actually stopped the construction of eight nuclear power units near Oak Ridge, the home of the atomic bomb, where the high school football team is called The Bombers. It was not easy. But, accountants killed nuclear power, not Jane Fonda."

At the TVA Freeman became a passionate advocate for public utilities, and he still is. Following his stint at TVA he headed the New York Power Authority, then the Lower Colorado River Authority, and then the Sacramento Municipal Utility District. But it was his remarkable service as the General Manager of the Los Angeles Department of Water and Power that brought him to the attention of Governor Davis and everyone else.

The City of Los Angeles owns its electric utility and simply calls it a department, like a police department. Remember that about 65 percent of electricity in the United States is provided by so-called investor-owned utilities, 20 percent is provided by municipal utilities, and 15 percent is provided by customer owned electrical cooperatives. These distinctions are not unimportant. The customers of municipally owned electric utilities routinely pay between 20 percent and 30 percent less for electricity than the customers of investor owned utilities. And so it is in Los Angeles. Imagine. If you live in Beverly Hills or Santa Monica you pay on average 25 percent more for electricity than folks living right down the street from you who happen to live in the City of Los Angeles.

And that isn't all.

In 1995 and 1996, California, like every place else, was caught up in the logic of electric deregulation and privatization. Almost all localities went along with deregulation, but Simon David Freeman's dedication to public power did not waiver and he talked Los Angeles mayor Richard Riordan and the city council out of adopting deregulation.

Fast forward to January 2001 and the now famous California electric brownouts. Because of Freeman's foresight and determination, the residents of the City of Los Angeles have a Kings X on electric brownouts. Not only do the folks in neighboring Santa Monica and Beverly Hills pay more for electricity, they now have brownouts while the TVs and refrigerators in Los Angeles hum. Thanks to Freeman, we have a world-class example of how government can do things right. Is it any wonder that Governor Davis tapped Simon David Freeman to lead California out of the darkness?

This is how Freeman feels about corporate or investor owned utilities like Southern California Edison and Pacific Gas and Electric: He suggests that, in the end, their responsibilities are to their stockholders. "I do think it is fair to say that the public power agencies continue to feel responsible for providing the power. Deregulation kind of leaves it up to Elvis Presley."

"It is time," he says, "that the words 'public power' are pronounced again in public. It was public power that turned the lights on in rural America. Not too many people are alive today who know that. We've had electricity in the whole country for 50 years, but not much more than that."

Freeman is not against corporate power and rejects suggestions that the power crisis has been caused by profiteering wholesalers and utilities in an effort to raise rates. "The stupidity theory explains most

61

things," he says. "Conspiracy theory doesn't work. We were just stupid in not thinking through how deregulation would work in a time of shortage."

Freeman is an outspoken advocate for energy conservation. One of his successes came at the Sacramento Municipal Utility District, which has one of the biggest solar and windmill power programs in the country. Sacramento has both low residential electric rates and a Kings X on brownouts.

Finally, Freeman exhibits one of the characteristics of the best public administrators—he sees the big picture and takes the long view. The future is not in big power—dams, nuclear power plants, and gigantic coal burning generators. The future is in micro-turbines, fuel cells, conservation, and clean power sources. Either way, Freeman says, the people really don't care how they get their electricity—until the lights go out. "I don't know many other issues in public policy, other than war, where everybody is affected. This is a very egalitarian problem. It's kind of like walking in the rain—it falls on everyone. Any fool can buy an umbrella on a rainy day. It takes a wise person to buy an umbrella on a sunny day."

If anyone can show California the way out of its electricity crisis it is Simon David Freeman.

A Real Hero

It is common to confuse greatness with notoriety in this era of celebrity. Even in public administration we too often substitute title and rank for importance. One of the responses to bureaucrat bashing has been the development of a literature on heroic or exemplary public servants, usually public servants at or near the top of their hierarchy. For public administration to have well-known bureaucratic heroes and examples has been helpful but may have missed a bigger point. To try to make that point let me tell you about a great public servant.

His name is Oscar Quail, and you do not know him. He is now

eighty-eight years old, a Twentieth Century man, a man of huge organizations and grand public purposes. A child of the West, in the 1930s he learned to ski before there were chair lifts, safety bindings, designer outfits and big lodges with stone fireplaces. He finished high school in the depth of the Depression and went to work. When the Second World War began he knew he would have to serve, and, sure enough, his draft notice arrived on his wedding day in 1942. Leaving his bride he was assigned to the Army ski training school at Iron Mountain, in the upper peninsula of Michigan. At the completion of his training and just before he was to ship out he was informed that he was to stay and be part of the staff teaching skiing to new recruits. His original unit shipped out, his place taken by a soldier who was later killed in Europe, as were several others in that unit. After the allied victory in Europe in 1944, there was no need for ski troops in the Pacific, so he was reassigned. After crossing the ocean on a crowded troop ship he was part of the Okinawa landing, his company hitting an empty beach. When the war was over, like millions of others, he came home to his wife and children, grateful that he had survived, and proud to have served his country. He was an enlisted man, a sergeant when discharged, just one tiny part of "the greatest generation," Tom Brokaw would later write about. He was neither a hero nor well known, just a typical GI who served his country, did his duty, and gave his country five years of his life.

And the country was grateful to Oscar Quail. With favorable mortgage arrangements made possible by the GI Bill he bought a little house in a modest neighborhood. He and Margaret still live there, the mortgage long since paid off. He got a job as a postman for the United States Post Office and joined the National Association of Letter Carriers. Day in and day out for over thirty years he delivered the mail, not on wheels but on foot. The mail was especially important in the days before e-mail and cell phones. In those days separated families kept in touch through the post. Oscar Quail carried the mail over his shoulder in heavy leather bags, from door to door, in good weather and bad. Once again he was just a tiny part of a huge organization, but an organization that knitted the country together, that facilitated the great engines of commerce, and that made us one.

He kept some of the family money in the Postal Saving program and borrowed money from the National Association of Letter Carriers Credit Union for cars and other big-ticket items. He received a fair but not lavish salary. His job was steady, orderly, reliable, and predictable. He had good benefits and because of his pension plan he and Margaret have had enough in their retirement. He raised three children and they now have grandchildren and great grandchildren.

Oscar Quail was devoted and loyal to the United States Army and the United States was loyal and devoted to him. He was devoted and loyal to the Post Office and the Post Office was devoted and loyal to him. He never aspired to managerial positions or to titles. He was content to be just one of tens of thousands like him who gave themselves to public service with the understanding that the federal government would be fair and just in return. And it was.

Will there be a generation of Oscar Quails in this era of downsizing, privatizing, contracting-out, part-time work, trimmed benefits, and bureaucrat bashing? Will we have a generation as loyal and dedicated to public service as Oscar Quail when there are growing questions about whether government will be loyal and dedicated to public servants? In the absence of a war which binds us together or great public purposes upon which we agree, can we no longer understand the necessity for large-scale governmental organizations and the need for loyal and dedicated public servants who work in them? Do we somehow imagine that we can get along without Oscar Quail? I hope not, because Oscar Quail is a public service hero.

Now bent over with age and from years of carrying the mail, Oscar cares for Margaret who is in the early stages of Alzheimer's. At least for now they are still in their little house, with their children nearby to help. Oscar Quail gave much of his life to serving the people, without praise or recognition, which makes his service all the more impressive. He perfectly represents the words engraved on the former Washington, D.C., City Post Office (now the site of the Smithsonian Institution's National Postal Museum.)

"The Post Office Department, in its ceaseless labors, pervades every channel of commerce and every theatre of human enterprise, and, while visiting, as it does kindly, every fireside, mingles with the throbbings of almost every heart in the land. In the amplitude of its beneficence, it ministers to all climes, and creeds, and pursuits, with the same eager readiness and equal fullness of fidelity. It is the delicate ear trump through which alike nations and families and isolated individuals whisper their joys and their sorrows, their convictions and their sympathies, to all who listen for their coming."

For over thirty years the grateful people on Oscar Quail's route "listened for his coming," and he never let them down. It was public service in its purest form.

Terrel Bell: Repositioning a Political Leader

The most enduring and important dilemma in public administration is this: how to be loyal to elected political leaders, yet adhere to professional and ethical standards. The best modern articulation of this dilemma is found in Albert Hirschman's theory of exit (to leave the agency if the policies or practices of political leaders are unacceptable), voice (to speak out on matters of policy or political practices), or loyalty (to accept and support the policies and practices of political leaders). Let me suggest a combination of Hirschman's voice and loyalty which I call "repositioning a political leader." Let me illustrate a reconciliation of the dilemma of political versus professional loyalty by "repositioning a political leader" with the remarkable case of Terrel H. Bell.

Ronald Reagan promised in his 1979 presidential campaign to get rid of the newly established U.S. Department of Education. After his election he appointed Terrel H. Bell of Utah as Secretary of Education, in part in return for strong political support in Utah and the other mountain states. After Bell's appointment the media had a generally good time ridiculing him for having taken over a department threatened with elimination. Six months after his appointment, a survey of Washington correspondents ranked Bell the least effective cabinet secretary. Yet three and one-half years later, in his campaign for reelection, President Reagan not only no longer wanted to eliminate the Department of Education, he wanted to lead a national movement to improve American schools. Ronald Reagan had been brilliantly repositioned by Terrel Bell.

This is how it happened.

Terrel Bell was a poor Idaho boy who hitchhiked to the Idaho State Normal School in Albion, the only college he could afford. He became a chemistry and physics teacher, served voluntarily in the Marines in World War II, returned to earn graduate degrees, after which he served as a school principal, district superintendent, and then a state commissioner of education. He served competently but unexceptionally as the U.S. Commissioner of Education in the old Department of Health, Education and Welfare in the Nixon and Ford administrations. A small, quiet and unpretentious man, Bell was regarded as a very good administrator and a tireless advocate for the public schools. His quiet manner and plain appearance lent credence to the negative media perception of him as a pliant participant in President Reagan's plan to eliminate the Department of Education.

Terrel Bell was a man easy to underestimate.

Shortly after taking office he met with the leaders of all the primary education professional associations and interest groups, and with large numbers of students, parents, teachers, and principals. These meetings confirmed his view that American public schools were in big trouble. He decided to establish a very high-level study to evaluate American schooling, and asked his friend David Gardner, then President of the University of California, to head it up. The National Commission on Excellence in Education included a sparkling array of leading Americans. The White House agreed that President Reagan would make the Commission appointments, but that it would not be a presidential commission. Commission funding had to be cobbled together.

The Commission study took just under two years. During this period the Reagan administration proposed sharply reduced budgets for the Department of Education while imploring their friends in Congress to support bills to eliminate the Department.

As the Commission went about its work, Bell carefully guided it in the direction of linking problems in American schooling to the declining competitiveness of American business in the global economy. In the end, the study made extensive and unfavorable comparisons of the standards and requirements of American as compared to Japanese, Korean, German, and other school systems.

Bell and Gardner chose the rather dramatic title, "A Nation at Risk" for the Commission report, which recommended that schools pay more attention to core subjects, set higher standards for students and teachers, and lengthen both the school day and the school year.

The full Commission gathered for the press conference for the public presentation of the report. The timing was exquisite at the height of national anxiety over Japanese competition, and just before the beginning of President Reagan's reelection campaign.

It was a bombshell, which dominated the news for weeks. An astonished Michael K. Deaver, President Reagan's political aide, told Bell that political polls were showing that the Commission report had caught the attention of the nation. Education was now a hot political topic and it was important for President Reagan to get out-in-front on the issue, which he did. Bell was transformed from a political pariah into an important cabinet member who now traveled with the president. There was no more talk of eliminating the Department of Education. Terrel Bell had taken Ronald Reagan to school.

Bell was so quiet, so unassuming and so willing to give others credit, that the Washington media never really caught on. When the flamboyant ideologue William Bennett was later appointed Secretary of Education he became a darling of the Chattering Classes, although little was accomplished during his tenure. In the years since Bell's tenure, the federal government has continued on the path of education reform, most notably with the passage of the No Child Left Behind legislation.

It was Terrel Bell who set the nation on the path of school reform and in the process reconciled his loyalty to the president and his deep commitment to the public schools. He did this gently by repositioning his political leader. He was of great service to his president and to his country.

Edward J. Curran: The Bureaucrat Who Would Not Be Bashed

Consider Edward J. Curran, the former head of counter-intelligence for the Department of Energy. Prior to these responsibilities he was an FBI agent for 37 years.

It was in a dust-up over espionage by the People's Republic of China that Mr. Curran achieved bureaucratic greatness. This is how it happened.

In matters such as these, cabinet officials and bureaucrats are ordinarily hauled onto the congressional turf where they are questioned, insulted, investigated, and generally punched about in what legislators grandly call hearings. But not the wily Mr. Curran. Instead, he chose to appear on the Sunday morning ABC "This Week" show with Cokie, Sam, the Two Georges (Stephanopolous and Will), and Irving Kristol's faithful son Bill. In this delightful contretemps, Mr. Curran described a 1997 report to Congress, which detailed the problem of Chinese espionage at the nuclear labs and even provided 26 specific recommendations for tightening security. He then said that Senator Richard C. Shelby (R-Alabama) failed to attend briefings where this report was presented and that the Senator's staff wouldn't accept the briefings and that they would "get up and walk away."

Mr. Curran also said he gave a report showing "very specific targeting of our cybernetwork within DoE by intelligence services" to the staff of Senator Frank H. Markowski (R-Alaska), Chairman of the Senate Energy and Natural Resources Committee, along with a request for $12.5 million to start dealing with the problem. Mr. Curran then indicated that the request for funding to improve security at DoE was rejected by Congress.

In a final act of bureaucratic bravery, Mr. Curran defended Attorney General Janet Reno who had been criticized by several legislators for failing to secure a warrant to get into the computer of the espionage suspect Wan Ho Lee who worked at the Los Alamo National Laboratory. Mr. Curran pointed out that DoE officials could not obtain a warrant, which would satisfy the legal requirements for "probable cause." He then said defiantly, "They're governed by the statutes. If Congress doesn't like this, then they should change the law."

It was an electric moment, a sabbath public administration epiphany, one of those rare and beautiful moments about which bureaucrats dream. In front of all America and in the presence of the leaders of the Chattering Classes, Mr. Curran made the bureaucratic equivalent of the winning field goal. He will forever be my hero.

The Chattering Classes loved it. Cokie said: "Well, we've had a rather remarkable morning.... Edward Curran, the FBI agent of 37 years, accused Congress of not paying enough attention to reports that were filed by him, and not paying attention to briefings on the whole question of security at nuclear labs.... He was very angry with the members of Congress."

Cokie then said: "George Stephanopolous, Bill Kristol, it was quite something here on the air. And you were all hearing things off the air as well. What were you hearing?"

George Stephanopolous replied: "Well, we were talking to Senator Torricelli and Senator Shelby outside, and they were outraged, I mean, just as they showed on the air. But Edward Curran was right. I mean, he briefed and the FBI briefed the Congress in 1996, the same time they briefed Sandy Berger, and there was no action. Now, everybody is shocked, shocked, shocked. But they weren't shocked a year and a half ago."

George Will then said: "The real offense of Mr. Curran was to criticize an elected member of Congress. And they just won't put up with that. And what he said, in effect, was, 'We were assigned to provide them with information. We did, and they were negligent about it.'"

Cokie then said: "You have him, and you have Notra Trulock, who was at the Department of Energy, ringing exactly the same alarm bells. Clearly, above them, both in the administration and in the Congress, there were people who just didn't want to hear it. They'd have to act on it. They'd have to do something. They'd have to spend some money. They'd have to pay attention."

Then George Will said: "I want to underscore that in the

Washington culture, we saw something extraordinary this morning and heroic. And whether or not Mr. Curran is punished remains to be seen."

Unaccustomed as they are to open criticism from public administrators, the Senators were outraged.

Senator Shelby said that Mr. Curran was "out of bounds on some areas."

Senator Torricelli said: "Mr. Curran knows better. I thought his comments were entirely inappropriate, particularly for someone in law enforcement."

Cokie Roberts then asked Senator Shelby why he had not been to all of the briefings and why his staff walked out, whereupon he replied: "Well, I certainly have not been to all of the briefings. But I've been to just about all the hearings. I've chaired all the hearings. And I have been at hearings where he was there. Oftentimes, they do brief the committee, the staffers that are dealing with counter-intelligence, if they're CIA, at the FBI, they brief the committee. They brief the top staffers on the committee because oftentimes we're not there."

Senator Torricelli then said: "I thought that as an executive official, his attacking the Congress and the intelligence committees of the Congress, in my judgment, did not respond appropriately. The Congress is also wanting in this. I don't think that the way to deal with this is for an FBI official now dealing with counter-intelligence to engage in a game of blame."

Blame indeed. It is evidently entirely appropriate for members of Congress to blame public administrators for the faults of government. But, for a bureaucrat to blame the Congress—now that is inappropriate.

Decades from now students will ask: "Who was this man Edward J. Curran, and why is he so important in public administration?"

Their professors will answer: "At the end of the 20th century, after decades of bureaucrat bashing by Congress, it was Edward J. Curran who would not be bashed. It was the beginning of the end of the political advantages that once came from bureaucrat bashing. It was Curran who demonstrated that it is acceptable for public administrators to openly speak truth to power."

Gloria Flora: Exit and Voice

Consider the resignation of Gloria Flora, the former Forest Supervisor of the Humboldt-Toiyabe National Forest in Nevada— the largest national forest in the lower 48 states. It would seem that the resignation of a single Fed is neither big news nor worthy of editorial comment. On the contrary. The Flora resignation is particularly important news especially deserving of the attention of everyone in public administration.

Gloria Flora was exactly what the best of public service should represent. She was a super grade (GS 15) with a distinguished 22-year federal career. Over the years she held and effectively carried out most of the top Forest Service leadership positions in the Western United States. In the bureaucratic world Gloria Flora was a superstar. Why, at age 44, in the midst of a brilliant career, would she resign?

Because she had the courage to say enough is enough.

The ostensible issue was the wild and native Dolly Varden trout, found only in Idaho, Oregon, and Nevada. In the watersheds in these states the beautiful Dolly Varden is either officially listed as endangered or is regarded as requiring "monitoring." Squeezed into a narrow and steep canyon of the Jarbridge River, near Jarbridge, Nevada (population 30), is an old 1.5 mile gravel road leading only to a wilderness trail head. Elko County claims to own this road although it is in the National Forest. At about mid-point the road washed out. After considerable deliberation the Forest Service decided to protect the gravel riverbed for Dolly Varden spawning and to advise Elko County not to rebuild the road but to work with them to locate the trailhead at the site of the washout.

Which brings us to the real issue.

The Elko County Commissioners used the road washout issue as a platform for a display of their radical form of states rights. They decided to send a bulldozer up the canyon to rebuild the road, which would have created 900 feet of slow moving warm water, which would be very harmful to the Dolly Varden. The State of Nevada ordered them to stop.

When a Nevada state assemblyman, John Carpenter, organized a volunteer group to rebuild the road, a federal judge issued a temporary restraining order for fear a confrontation between officials of the Forest Service and the volunteers would turn violent. In the meantime, the U.S. Fish and Wildlife Service has rebuilt the riverbed at considerable expense.

The Jarbridge road washout issue is a skirmish in the Sagebrush Rebellion, a long-standing effort by rural Nevada ranchers and others who claim that the federal government (they refer to the federal government as the occupying government) does not have a legitimate right to decide matters of cattle grazing, road building, mining, or mineral and oil exploration in the West. Over the past 20 years employees of the Forest Service and the Bureau of Land Management have been vilified, intimidated, threatened, denied food in restaurants and rooms in motels, had their children ridiculed in school, and their offices bombed.

Having served in the West her entire career, Gloria Flora was a seasoned veteran of the Sagebrush Rebellion. Skirmishes such as the Jarbridge road washout were nothing new. But what happened next was simply too much.

Former representatives Helen Chenoweth-Hage (R-Idaho), and Jim Gibbons (R-Nevada) announced congressional hearings on the Jarbridge matter and other matters, to be held in Elko in late November. The list of those who were to testify included employees of the Forest Service and the Bureau of Land Management and "experts," almost all of whom are critics of federal government ownership and control of western land. But even that was not unusual; such hearings are often a kind of public grandstanding for political purposes. This list of witnesses, however, included the personal attorney of Wayne Hage, Representative Chenoweth-Hage's husband who has a 10 year history of defying the federal government on his extensive land holdings in Nevada. Hage was, at the time, suing the Forest Service for $26 million, a suit that later failed. The blatant conflict of interest was simply too much. In addition, the hearings were to be followed by a fundraiser for Chenoweth-Hage and Gibbons! It was clear that federal government employees were to be the public punching bags for Representatives Chenoweth-Hage and Gibbons prior to their fund-raiser.

Gloria Flora decided that she would have none of it. In a letter to her supervisors in the Forest Service she resigned as the Supervising Forester for the Humbolt-Toiyabe National Forest.

When I spoke with her on the telephone, here are some of the things she said.

First, this was a high-profile resignation to underscore the significance of issues associated with the open and sanctioned mistreatment of federal civil servants. She simply could no longer stand by and not speak out for all of the employees under her supervision in Nevada.

Second, there are only a few things that draw attention to such issues—bombings, killings (one thinks of Oklahoma City), or high-profile resignations. She could not openly criticize elected officials and still supervise the forest. So she chose to be openly critical.

Third, she pointed out that Representative Chenoweth-Hage had a glaring conflict of interest in the hearings.

Representative Chenoweth-Hage met with the Elko County Commissioners to advise them on how to fight the Forest Service.

Flora would have welcomed a serious and fair hearing but she would not subject either herself or her employees to a political circus.

I asked her if her Forest Service career was over. She said it was not. She has had strong expressions of internal support and has received over a dozen cards and letters from retired Forest Service employees. She has been assured that a suitable Forest Service position in a suitable place will be available. In fact, that is highly unlikely.

She did indicate that there were some expressions of "concern" on the part of some of her supervisors over her comment to a reporter that Representative Chenoweth-Hage had a conflict of interest.

Gloria Flora was a courageous and dedicated public service professional. No government employee should have to experience what she and her fellow federal employees who work in Nevada have experienced. In a general sense it is inappropriate for a civil servant to publicly question an elected official. And, it is altogether appropriate for an elected official to seek to change the laws and the policies and to hold hearings to discuss the laws and the policies. But it is absolutely wrong for elected officials to publicly abuse civil servants and to aid and abet those who intimidate and threaten them. When that happens or is about to happen it is right for civil servants to vigorously defend themselves and to do so publicly. It is also right for civil servants under such circumstances to point out when hearings and other systems of legislative oversight are abusive or insulting.

Well done, Gloria Flora.

Joseph Santos Ileto: A Citizen Twice

Let me tell you about Joseph Santos Ileto. He was the oldest in a family of five children who immigrated with their parents to the United States in 1974 from the Philippines. Joseph was fourteen. The Ileto family settled in Southern California where, like millions of immigrants before them, they worked hard for a share of the American dream. Joseph graduated from Schurr High School in Montebello, a working class city just south of Los Angeles. He attended East Los Angeles Community College where he studied engineering. He was cheerful, friendly and popular. He was especially fond of competitive table games and developed into an excellent chess player, regularly participating in chess tournaments in Southern California.

To make ends meet, Joseph had two jobs, one as a part-time employee of the United States Postal Service where he covered the mail delivery routes for other postal workers who had time off. He was competent, pleasant and very reliable, a quality of special importance to the Postal Service.

On August 10th, Joseph Santos Ileto was delivering the mail in Chatsworth when a car pulled up next to him and the driver asked him if he would mail a letter. Joseph said yes. The driver then stepped out of his car and shot Joseph point blank in the front of his body. As Joseph turned and fell, the killer fired seven additional shots into his back. (I do not use the name of the killer on purpose. He does not deserve to be mentioned by name in story about Joseph Santos Ileto.) An hour earlier the killer shot five people, including three children and a grandmother, at a Jewish community center. They all survived. According to an interview affidavit, the killer said he chose Joseph Santos Ileto to shoot because he was a person of color and because he worked for government.

The motives of the killer appeared to be essentially the same as those who plotted and carried out the bombing of the Murrah Federal Building in Oklahoma City. So, we add the name of Joseph Santos Ileto to the list of those in Oklahoma City who were killed because they were working for government.

Like the dead of Oklahoma City, Joseph Santos Ileto was a citizen twice. He was himself a good, honest, hard-working American citizen. But he was also a citizen again, working for us all, a citizen in lieu of us, doing what needed to be done so that we can all reach for the American dream. And he died in our service, a citizen twice.

It was Winston Churchill who first used the phrase citizens twice. In the early stages of World War II, the British were in France fighting with the French against the German invasion. They were driven to Dunkirk on the French coast of the English Channel and were desperately attempting to get across the Channel to safety. It soon became evident that the British navy and merchant marine was so seriously depleted that they could rescue only a small percentage of the trapped army. Urgent messages were sent to anyone with access to a boat asking them to volunteer to assist in an evacuation. Soon there appeared a remarkable armada of pleasure boats, fishing boats, coastal ferries, coal haulers, and merchant ships sailing back and forth across the Channel, in the face of German submarines and coastal guns, to rescue almost all of an estimated 100,000 people.

After the dramatic rescue, Churchill went to the towns and villages of the Channel coast and thanked those brave civilians who participated in the rescue. He called them citizens twice.

Joseph Santos Ileto was a modern-day citizen twice.

75

Book Four
Modern Public Organization and Management

Look, Public Administration Ain't Rocket Science

In our day, the standard against which the relative difficulty or complexity of a task is measured is the claim that it is easier than rocket science. It seems that rocket science, and particularly putting men on the moon and bringing them back, is thought to be the greatest of our achievements. The earliest expression of the special place of rocket science in the pantheon of great human accomplishments was the 1970s phrase, "If we can land a man on the moon, why can't we solve the problems of the ghetto?" In a country of vast resources, wealth and technology, why can't we provide medical care at a reasonable cost to all who need it; keep the streets, air, and water clean; reduce crime; educate ghetto kids; provide decent and low-cost mass transport; halt the rise in housing and service costs.

The brilliant economist Richard R. Nelson wrote those words many years ago and described the moon-ghetto metaphor, or the continuing comparison of all other human tasks to space travel in his book *The Moon and the Ghetto*. With the help of H. Ross Perot, the moon-ghetto metaphor has evolved to the trite but persistent contemporary phrase "look, this (public administration, or insert your own subject) ain't rocket science." For the reasons that follow, I ask you to join me in a pledge to never use "look, this ain't rocket science" again, to leave the company of anyone else using that phrase, and to excuse yourself from any gathering at which such a phrase is uttered. By acting together, we can stamp out this insult to our collective intelligence.

First, rocket science has proven to be somewhat less than entirely reliable. It is my guess that rocket scientists themselves, as a way to dim the spotlight on their recent errors, would prefer the phrase "look, this ain't cell biology," or "look, this ain't theoretical physics."

Second, in his analysis of the moon-ghetto metaphor, Richard R. Nelson reminds us that we get approximately what we pay for—he is an economist after all. For example, we have a huge interstate highway system and each American metropolitan area has an elaborate system of highways and roads. But, with the exception of a few metropolitan areas, we do not have viable public transportation systems. We have invested in highways and cars but not in urban mass transit. We have also invested heavily in space travel and exploration. After the Columbia accident, NASA pointed out that they are spending less money on each mission than they have in the past, implying that less money results in lower reliability. But it isn't just money. It is also political will. Paul Light's wonderful book, *Government's Greatest Achievements: From Civil Rights to Homeland Security*, is a compilation and elaboration of successful programs (safe food and water, public education, the right to vote, financial and health security for the elderly, etc.) in which we have invested either our financial resources or our political will.

Third, certain fields of human endeavor display an orderliness that lends itself to scientific precision and measurement and to the development of rules, laws, and principles. Cell biology is like that and so is the physics of space travel. While technically challenging (we have yet to find the cure for cancer), such orderly human endeavors also lend themselves to management. Other fields of human endeavor, while not random, are much less orderly and, therefore, less amenable to scientific precision and to management. There is simply no question that building more freeways is much easier than figuring out how to improve inner-city public education. Constructing freeways that do not get potholes seems, however, to have evaded the highway builders.

Some years ago Erwin C. Hargrove and John C. Glidewell captured these issues in *Impossible Jobs in Public Management*. All jobs vary along several dimensions of difficulty, but some jobs fall at the difficult extreme of so many dimensions that they can legitimately be called impossible. The dimensions of job impossibility have to do with the extent to which there is public agreement regarding what needs to be done (for example, should prisons be for punishment or for rehabilitation?) and the relative legitimacy of an agency's clients (should unemployed single mothers be required to work in order to receive welfare?). "Impossible" describes public responsibility for which a level of success is ordinarily rather low (successful prison rehabilitation, successful inner-city schools, etc.) compared to possible jobs, or, to put it bluntly, easier jobs. Space travel and rocket science, it turns out, are more possible and easier.

Here are some public organizational questions that make rocket science look easy. How shall we update and improve the electricity transmission grid in the context of a "not in my back yard" public? How shall we deal with drug abuse without filling our prisons to the bursting point? How shall we contain the rising costs of health care, including pharmaceuticals? How shall we improve inner-city public schooling in the context of poverty, crime, and seriously frayed families? How shall we equalize social and governmental costs and benefits in governmentally fragmented metropolitan areas with poor inner cities and wealthier suburbs? And, with every supposed answer to each of these questions, comes the next question—who will pay for it?

I doubt very much whether rocket science has anything of consequence to contribute to the answers to these questions. So, let us drop the "look, this ain't rocket science" phrase and insist that others do the same. And while we are at it, let's also drop these phrases: think outside the box; at the end of the day; bottom line; win-win; strategic fit; 24/7; and results-driven.

The elimination of these phrases will, all by themselves, significantly improve public administration.

Public Sector High Reliability

It wasn't just the Y2K problem that didn't happen. Something probably much more important didn't happen either. Because what didn't happen is not news, we missed it entirely.

In any given year between the beginning of the Thanksgiving holiday and the end of the Christmas/Hanukkah/New Year's holidays, a period of 40 days, approximately 50 million people take commercial scheduled air flights. That is nearly 14 percent of the entire population of the United States! Any late afternoon and evening during this 40-day period there were just under 500,000 people hurtling through the sky at 500 miles per hour, at the same time, traveling in all directions, entirely safely. Not one person died in regularly scheduled commercial air travel.

During this same period electricity generated by nuclear, gas, oil, hydro, and coal systems, kept 100 million American homes lit, powered our cooking and cleaning utilities, and lit the television sets we watched to see the celebrations of the year 2000 sweep across the earth. All of this happened because nothing went wrong.

The hospitals operated, the natural gas supply system heated our homes and our water, the 911 system operated smoothly, our food and medicine was safe and reliable, the communication satellites stayed in orbit, there were no terrorist incidents. Nothing happened!

Nothing bad happened because all of our high reliability systems worked just perfectly, or at least well enough. If any one of these systems had failed it is likely that our problems would have been at least as serious as the potential problems associated with Y2K. Breakdowns in our high reliability systems such as Three Mile Island, Egypt Air, and Value Jet are remembered vividly. It seems ordinary and routine when high reliability systems work properly, but when they fail it is news and often news that milks the incident well beyond its importance.

It is perhaps useful to remember that one hundred years ago in the transition between 1899 and 1900 none of these systems even existed. What we now enjoy as a result of these high reliability systems would seem miraculous to those who witnessed that transition, but to us such miracles are so ordinary and routine that we are short tempered with the slightest variation in system reliability.

Tucked away in the recesses of public administration research and theory is a little storehouse of very useful information about these high reliability systems. The scholarly work of Martin Landau, Todd La

Porte, Paula Consolini, David Sills, Louise Comfort, Joseph Morone and Edward Woodhouse, Charles Perrow, James Reason, and Karl Weick has all contributed to this storehouse of knowledge. To summarize and simplify, here is what we know about high reliability systems and why they work.

High reliability systems use a much different logic when compared with trial-and-error, failure-tolerant systems. The incremental, mixed scanning, loose coupling, resource scarcity, and bounded rationality theories—theories that explain much of standard organizational behavior—are replaced in high reliability systems with the following:

First, the physical technologies (radar, nuclear generating plants, and so forth) of these systems are tightly coupled, which is to say that an important breakdown anywhere along the production process may cause the whole system to fail.

Second, this tight coupling is characterized by fixed and relatively rigid standard operating procedures or procedure protocols that do not ordinarily vary, which is to say that administrative discretion is sharply reduced.

Third, humans operating along any point in the production process of high reliability systems require extensive technological training and constant retraining.

Fourth, such systems are ordinarily funded to a level that will guarantee high efficiency, or, put differently, efficiency is much more important than economy in the world of high reliability.

Fifth, such systems are highly redundant, with two, three, or even four backup or redundant systems if the primary system were to fail. One thinks immediately of the redundancy that saved the Apollo 13 space mission.

Sixth, such systems are highly networked, which is to say that many different organizations are in the production chain. Consider, for example, air travel, which involves at least the following in a tightly coupled network: the Federal Aviation Administration; air traffic controllers; local airport managers; commercial airline companies including the pilots, attendants, and so forth; airline manufacturers, the airline maintenance companies; fuel suppliers.

Seventh, these systems are composed of a marvelous mix of governmental, nongovernmental, and commercial organizations, the very definition of high-functioning public-private partnerships.

Eighth, when working properly, error reporting is encouraged and not punished; indeed, initiatives to identify flaws in procedures and protocols and thereby avoid failure are rewarded.

Ninth, ordinarily such systems are rather hierarchical, both within the system and within the organization making up the system. But at times of peak load and emergencies one finds rule switching by which officials move away from hierarchy and procedures to seek the expertise or experience that might account for or explain an anomaly and provide suggestions for possible non-routine solutions. One thinks again of the Apollo 13 space mission.

These failure-free systems reveal how remarkably effective modern public and private organizations can be if they have adequate resources and are well managed. To be sure, failure-free systems are the subject of intense public scrutiny because of the visibility of failures, however rare. Such systems are also a great favorite of alarmists, however well meaning. One thinks of a former Inspector General of the Federal Aviation Administration so determined to show how unsafe air travel is that she tried to pass through an airport security system with dangerous things in her carry-on luggage. She was caught.

There will be failure and there will be accidents; simple probability demonstrates that it is so. But on a day-to-day basis we all enjoy the modern miracles of high reliability systems. And, interestingly, when they fail it is usually because of human fallibility.

It is difficult to imagine modern life without high reliability systems. When they work perfectly, it appears that nothing happens. In fact, everything happens properly.

High Reliability and Freedom from Terror

Freedom from terror would not ordinarily be included among our cherished Bill of Rights freedoms such as free assembly, privacy, and a free press. Since September 11th, however, freedom from terror is at the top of that list and, as in the case of our other precious freedoms, we turn to government to guarantee it.

It is helpful to think of freedom from terror as a pure public good, not divided up easily or available in the marketplace. For example, the blessings that come from the absence of war are shared approximately equally—I do not get more protection from national defense than you do. Freedom from terror is like that.

Pure public goods tend to be governmental monopolies such as law enforcement, fire protection, prisons and jails, water and sanitation services. We could all hire bodyguards and drink bottled water, but most of us don't because we rely on government to provide these protections. Freedom from terror is like that too.

The effectiveness of pure public goods can be difficult to measure. Although we know it is valuable, what value should be assigned to the relative absence of violent crime? After September 11th we know how valuable freedom from terror really is, and we are willing to dedicate to it the things we cherish—our time, our money, our creativity, possibly some of our privacy and, for some, our lives. Like many other things of great worth—love, family, patriotism, security, and peace—freedom from terror is tough to measure.

Finally, freedom from terror has this unique characteristic: Like crime, water and air pollution, and war, terror is best understood by its absence. For such public services as education, we count on government to cause things to happen—to build schools, hire teachers, develop curricula, teach, and so forth. In the case of terrorism, we count on government to cause things not to happen, to prevent terror.

Considering freedom from terror from the perspective of a pure public good brings us to these three vexing questions: How shall we organize and manage to effectively prevent terror? How shall we know when terror is prevented? How shall we measure the value of terror that did not to happen?

Terrorism is global but manifests itself locally, not fitting standard governmental and organizational distinctions between things international and things domestic. Like many other problems, the disconnect between terrorism in its many possible forms and the complex structure of American government is painfully evident. Although it may be trite, in the case of terrorism this adage is apt: The people have problems; the government has departments. Certainly the cabinet level Department of Homeland Security will help to better connect the problems of terrorism to the departments of government. The key word here is "connect." The emphasis shall be on building the right connections between the capacities of government found in dozens of departments, agencies, and bureaus, including state and local governments, and focusing those capacities on terrorism.

Assuming the continued organizational complexity of American government, the management challenges that are associated with terrorism are usefully informed by our knowledge of high reliability systems such as the operation of nuclear power plants, nuclear submarines and aircraft carriers, and air travel. High reliability systems, while subject to the statistical probability of so-called normal accidents, are incredibly effective for the following reasons. First, such systems are multiorganizational and operate on the basis of very high organizational interdependence, a form of intense coordination usually described as tight coupling. Participants operate on the basis of agreed-upon protocols that are strictly followed. Second, there is equally tight coupling between organizational technologies (airplanes, radar detectors, baggage scanners, etc.) and the humans who operate these technologies. Third, training is intense and continual. Fourth, reporting possible system error is highly valued rather than punished. Fifth, there are at least three levels of system redundancy. Sixth, in the interest of high reliability, funding is adequate or better. Seventh, at both the organizational and the system level, there is a forthright pursuit of knowledge of possible sources of system failure (in the case of terrorism this is usually called intelligence).

Within the framework of law, all necessary steps are taken to disable possible sources of system failure. Given the varied nature of terrorism, such as bioterrorism, low tech truck bombings, agriterrorism, and airplane hijacking, the particulars of effective high reliability systems will also vary. Given the varied nature of terrorism, an effective response will require great managerial and administrative creativity and unprecedented levels of cooperation between connected organizations.

If antiterrorism high reliability systems work we will know it by the absence of terrorism. This is a problem in an era in which it is thought that the effectiveness of all government services can be annually measured. Measurement of goal achievement is always difficult for pure public goods, and it is especially difficult for antiterrorism. How is a local police department or a state department of public health to measure its part of a tightly coupled antiterrorist system when it is impossible to know what part of effective antiterrorism might have been contributed by these agencies? The logic of tight coupling can help to determine the gaps in a comprehensive antiterrorism program, and cooperating organizations can work together to fill those gaps.

Certain things can and must be measured, such as the level of training, the understanding of protocols, organizational effectiveness in drills and simulations, and progress in filling system gaps. These are process measures, and in high reliability systems such processes are critically important. But processes are not results.

The Department of Justice and the Federal Bureau of Investigation, in accord with the Government Performance and Results Act, developed a strategic plan including efforts to "deter and detect terrorist incidents by developing maximum intelligence and investigative capability." The specific goals under this plan are to prevent terrorist acts and protect critical infrastructure, and to improve response capabilities to terrorists' acts. The measures of performance include the number of terrorist cases investigated, the number of terrorists convicted, and the number of terrorist acts prevented. For the current fiscal year the measure of the number of terrorist acts prevented has been discontinued because "the measure varies considerably from year to year, is wholly subject to external factors, and does not demonstrate any sort of predictive value about the condition of defense against terrorism in the U.S."

Well said. Since September 11th, Justice and the FBI must be judged on the basis of cooperation, tight coupling, creative intelligence gathering, training, and building redundancies in conjunction with others. These are processes that can and should be measured. But, like many other pure public goods, the ultimate measure of the effectiveness of a systemic approach to antiterrorism is when terrorism does not happen and we are free from terror.

Terrorism: The Folly of Experience and the Wisdom of History

American public administration is uniquely a product of the 20th century, indeed the history of modern American public administration roughly parallels the history of 20th century American government. By any measure the study and practice of public administration has been a success, contributing importantly to virtually all significant American public achievements.

Our direct collective experience began at mid-century, just after digging out of the Great Depression and winning the second World War. By then it was clear that this was to be the American Century. And it was equally clear that it was positive government that had secured American success at home and our standing abroad. This was the experience of our parents.

In our somewhat more direct experience we have had two essentially unsuccessful wars, Korea and Vietnam, and several relatively minor dust-ups. In our immediate experience we fought brief wars in Panama, the Persian Gulf, Bosnia, Kosovo, and Iraq. The regional wars of the past 50 years have not required national mobilization and we even discontinued the system of mandatory military service that evened out the probability of sacrifice. During much of that 50-year period, military policy was guided by the logic of the cold war—the control of Communist expansion and nuclear deterrence. By the end of the 20th century Soviet Communism collapsed and Chinese Communism, while still totalitarian, is moving increasingly from a socialist to a market platform. The military successes of the past 50 years, to use a phrase from the Vietnam era, have been accomplished without giving up butter for guns. We now live in a world in which the United States is the dominant military power.

The last 50 years of the American economy too have been a success, at least for the majority of us. There has been no depression, family incomes have increased as has per-worker productivity. A good bit of the increase in family income growth, however, can be traced to the sharply increased percentage of women in the work force. From the mid-1970s to the mid-1990s there was no real growth in per-worker income when that income is discounted for inflation and particularly the growth in health care costs. The American middle class has grown significantly as has the level of home ownership. At the end of the century we are experiencing low inflation, real growth in worker income, and the lowest unemployment in decades.

In general terms American health is the best it has ever been. The issue is not the quality of health and healthcare but the quality of health and healthcare for whom. Again the benefits of long life and good health are by no means equal being largely determined by economic status. Still, the general capacity of the American healthcare system, even with its quirky reliance on insurance companies and managed care systems, is solid.

The high reliability systems that bring us electricity and gas, that vouchsafe air travel, that see to the safety and quality of our food and medicine and provide for instantaneous communication are little short of miraculous. We rely on them so entirely that we are ill-tempered in the face of the slightest breakdown.

In virtually all fields of American public policy—housing, schooling, healthcare, transportation, public safety, communication, natural resources management, food production, environmental quality—the past 50 years has written success stories. Judged from the perspective of public policy these years have resulted in the highest quality of life in the world's history, the envy of much of the rest of the world.

But the experiences of the past 50 years have also taught us other things. Virtually all our primary institutions—family, church, neighborhood, professions, schools, health care institutions, media, and particularly government—have diminished in public regard and have suffered significant losses in individual and collective support. It is as if we have somehow agreed that people, individuals, are good and important, but that our institutions are bad. Arguments for reform of institutions fill the air, as if to say that by fixing our institutions we can fix ourselves.

The experiences of these decades appear to have taught us to disinvest in our institutions and invest in ourselves. In the governmental sector this takes the form of the political slogans: "Government is not the solution, government is the problem," and "The era of big government is over." Such slogans appear to make good sense and have proven to be very good politics, given the people's mood at the century's end.

The essential lesson we have learned from the blessings of the past 50 years, blessings at least partially resting on the foundations of the positive state, is that we must be significantly less invested in and reliant on large-scale governmental institutions and programs. The foundation upon which 21st century public administration rests is one of weakened and fragmented institutions, the increasingly disarticulated state, and a remarkable collective hubris regarding our capacity to manage our way through the coming years.

To see the future of American public administration as a linear extrapolation of our direct and learned experience, the experiences of the past 50 years would suggest that downsizing, privatizing, deregulating, contracting, load shedding, performance measuring, benchmarking, report carding, marketing, and the other management fashions of the day are here to stay. With these concepts we have built the foundation of 21st century public administration and we will never look back. Let me gently suggest such an imagined 21st century public administration is hubris and folly, and the best evidence of this is the terrorism of September 11, 2001.

To put that terrorism in context, reflect on the experiences of the past 50 years as the basis for preparing for the 21st century, and consider instead the last full century of American public administration history. In the first two decades of the 20th century we experienced the First World War and an influenza epidemic, both resulting in great loss of life and extensive public mobilization and institutionalization. In the third and fourth decades of the 20th century we saw race and poor riots and the Great Depression. So, we called even more on the positive state and invested even further in our public institutions. In the fifth decade, we fought the Second World War, requiring almost total public mobilization including extensive regulation and massive borrowing. Our public institutions responded remarkably well, using the logic of classic public administration—the principals of management, POSDCORB, the politics-administration dichotomy, budgeting theory, civil service logic, and all the rest. We learned how to respond to large-scale threat, crisis, disaster, and emergency. By the sixth decade, the institutions of the positive state were revered and those who worked in them were respected. Most of our social and political institutions enjoyed a broad legitimacy.

From a historical perspective the question is this: Which half of the American 20th century was aberrant? Any serious understanding of the cycles and rhythms of history would lead to the conclusion that it was the last half of the century that was aberrant. The lessons learned by those of us who have directly experienced only the last five decades of the 20th century are misleading and possibly even dangerous, particularly in light of September 11th.

A wise person once uttered this truism: "Yesterday's solutions have become today's problems." Even if it is not always true or is only partially true, the elements of the new managerialism we now embrace will render vulnerable the public sector generally and public administration particularly. And this is likely to come to pass even without future disaster, tragedy, war, depression, or epidemic.

The lessons of history teach us that there will certainly be economic reversals, the only questions are how severe, how long, and how often. Will the public administration foundation based on the logic of the new managerialism hold up under conditions of terrorism, depleted retirement funds, and the widening gap between the rich and the poor? Under such circumstances will deregulated businesses and government contractors be public spirited and pick up the slack?

We also learn from history the likelihood of war, and war on a larger scale than we have recently experienced. With the demise of the Soviet Union the probability of full scale world war is probably reduced. But regional conflict and in some cases rather large scale regional conflict as the war in Iraq are more likely.

The real reason we have diminished institutions and declining respect for them can be traced to circumstances. Because American circumstances and conditions have been so generally favorable in the past 50 years, we simply have needed our institutions less. Without big problems we have not needed big government. We could also openly glorify self-interest. The circumstances and conditions of the first 50 years of the 20th century were filled with big problems requiring big institutional responses. We were willing to mobilize, sacrifice and find consensus in our collective pursuit of high purposes. As we end the century there are few big problems and still fewer high purposes.

How will public administration respond now that the country is faced with terrorism? How should we prepare for a really challenging contingency?

The lesson is this: Events, circumstances, and times change, but the core values of public administration are constant. We must understand how to effectively deliver public services and we must trust in our representative form of democratic self-government. In the present arid landscape of diminished institutions, management fads, policy gimmicks, and leadership rhetoric, we must return to our core values and practices. We must be as prepared as we are able for terrorism and other serious problems, for such serious problems will surely come. The best of modern public administration will not be overly enthralled by the set of modern practices built to manage diminished institutions, but will be informed by a longer history which includes a public administration practiced in the context of the positive and consensual state.

Terrorism and Air Passenger Safety

It is now clear that the September 11th terrorists had spent months and perhaps years planning the hijacking of commercial airlines for the purpose of flying them into the World Trade Center and the Pentagon. Based on extensive travel though airports on the east coast and careful observation of airport security, the terrorists chose Boston's Logan airport as their point of departure, evidently because of its particularly lax security. What is it about Logan airport that might explain why it was attractive to airplane hijacking terrorists?

Local airports are organized in two ways. Of the top 30 commercial airports, according to Spencer Dickerson, executive vice president of the International Association of Airport Executives, 10 are simply city departments of aviation, like departments of public works. The other 20 are semi-autonomous authorities (special districts) either established by cities or by combinations of cities, counties, and/or states. Of the top 30 airports, all are, they claim, self-supporting, deriving their revenues from runway and gate fees charged to airlines, parking, vendor contracts, and the like. Airports are responsible for all security except passenger and luggage screening, which was the responsibility of the airlines, and is now being federalized.

Boston's Logan Airport is the primary facility of a Massachusetts state level authority called Massport. Governed by a board of directors appointed by the governor, Massport was established many years ago as a semi-autonomous authority presumably to insulate it from politics and to enable it to function like a business.

Following September 11th, Jane Swift, then governor of Massachusetts, appointed a Special Advisory Task Force on Massport with instructions to do a thorough review of the agency and to report back in 45 days with findings and recommendations. Here they are.

- Massport should hire an experienced airport professional as its CEO. Ordinarily such a recommendation would deserve a yawn, but not in Massachusetts. Virginia Buckingham, who was the CEO on September 11th and has now resigned, was a public relations staff person for Governors Weld and Cellucci, with no background in airport management. She followed Peter Blute, a former state legislator and U.S. congressman who resigned as Massport CEO after being photographed on a "booze cruise" in Boston Harbor with less then fully clothed young ladies. It turns out that Governor Swift herself is also a former public relations person who had once served on the Massport senior staff as a result of political patronage. So, while professional qualifications might be assumed for most important public administration responsibilities elsewhere, requiring actual qualifications for those in the leadership of Logan Airport in Boston would be a very big change.

- There should also be professional qualifications for a new position, airport Chief of Security. It turns out that there are presently no such requirements, and the former Massport Public Safety Director, Joseph M. Lawless (I did not make this up), had no professional background in airport security.

- Patronage at Massport, "in all of its forms," should be eliminated. "We conclude that patronage at Massport is a four headed monster, taking the following forms: the hiring of unqualified individuals, the creation of new positions to accommodate applicants, the awarding of contracts to companies with inside connections, and financial contributions to charities or outside parties that go beyond community goodwill."

If there is a person who knows governmental affairs in Massachusetts and Boston it is Robert H. (Tex) McClain, Jr., a lifetime member (and former president) of ASPA. According to McClain, the description of Massport patronage as a four headed monster is no exaggeration. Massport is, he says, corrupt like many cities were before the progressive era and the municipal reform movement. But, rather than a boss mayor, Massport is a political extension of the governor and the governor's political party. The Task Force report reads: "The blame for patronage not only rests with the leadership of Massport; it rests equally with other political entities, including the Executive and Legislative branches of government, among others, which, without regard for technical and professional qualifications or fairness, have frequently used this public agency as a vehicle for political reward." It is estimated that at least 25 percent of Massport employees can trace their jobs to patronage.

The Massport budget is larded-up with pork including the favored charities of political worthies, and capitol projects in the districts of the influential. Read this and shudder: "In an odd way, the Authority is proud of how it has coped with patronage. Paying for problems to go away by accommodating high level hires on the payroll, by creating special positions in the organization, or spending $1.4 million to fund the preferred charities of influential people seems to be an acceptable compromise in the short run to win consensus."

- Massport is poorly organized and managed. It is "overstaffed, particularly at the top levels of administration. There is also duplication of function, excessive layers of middle management, and lack of access to the CEO by the managers of the core functions."

According to McClain, the logic of Massport as a semi-autonomous authority has neither insulated it from politics nor resulted in good business practices. It is the worst of both worlds—poor government and lousy business.

For the past 75 years city airports have been vital partners in the American commercial air travel system. The safety of air travel is the net result of close and carefully designed linkages between airports, airline companies, fuel and other supply companies, maintenance companies, the FAA, and many other partners. If one of the partners in the airport security system fails to properly carry out its responsibilities, the whole system is compromised. We will never know how much of the responsibility for September 11th can be fairly associated with organization and management of Boston's Logan Airport. But, it is good to know that they now have a blueprint for reform, reform based on public administration principles such as professional qualifications, the clear assignment of responsibilities, a chain of command, and, above all, a distinct line between politics and administration.

The Latest in Privatization and Contracting

Add this to your list of very good things to read: Elliott D. Sclar, *You Don't Always Get What You Pay For: The Economics of Privatization* and add to the names of the intellectual leaders of the study of contracting out—Donald Kettl, Lester Salamon, Brinton Milward and Keith Provan, Barbara Romzek and Jocelyn Johnston, Steven Smith and Michael Lipsky, Paul Light, and Joel Handler—the name Elliott Sclar.

Sclar does public administration a considerable favor by cutting through the use and abuse of words. In Europe and much of the rest of the world privatization means exactly that, selling to private businesses government owned railroads, coal and iron mines, airlines, collective farms, and big industrial plants. In the United States such privatization rarely happens although there have been a few advocates of selling the Tennessee Valley Authority or the Atlanta airport.

Compared to other countries, government activities in the United States have always been circumscribed, therefore, there are few public goods to sell.

Instead, corporations and nonprofit institutions are doing an increasing percentage of the work of American government through contracts. Because of the political popularity of the word "privatization," our elected leaders have come to call contracting out privatization and public administration has dutifully followed. So, Sclar, let it be loud and clear—privatization in the United States is not actually privatization, it is the contracting out of government services.

Sclar's work, supported by the Century Foundation (formerly the Twentieth Century Fund), is based on richly detailed cases of actual privatization and how it works.

Consider these several verses in the privatization scriptures:

Privatization saves money. Some years ago I wrote that in government, as in most things, you get what you pay for. It was probable, I argued, that a government that costs less is a government that either does less or does what it presently does less well. Elected officials, journalists and consultants regarded this contention as heresy and badly out-of-step with the times. My academic friends said that I could be right but that I was spitting into a mighty wind. Contracting would, its prophets claimed, do the work of government better and for less. The years have passed, we now have more experience with contracting out, and we now have Sclar's research. Comparative cost studies do not, Sclar finds, yield unambiguous evidence of contracts saving money and that, "there are clearly situations in which contracting works well, [but] there are many, if not more, in which the existence of direct public service is a rational economic strategy."

Privatization takes advantage of market competition. Sclar's words are far better than mine. "Viewed in the light of the textbook theory of perfect competition, privatization is effectively advocated as a process of wholesale remote-control organizational change.... [P]roponents of this view of privatization promise a quick, easy, and almost dreamlike solution to all that ails public service. They exhibit a fundamentalist faith in the imminent arrival of a level of competition that always proves to be just beyond reach. Lost in the crusade is any substantial understanding of the systemic, and largely economic, forces which shape contemporary public work and limit the effectiveness of public contracting." There are many reasons why market competition seldom applies in the public sector. Sclar reviews them all in his cases, and concludes that competition is a weak rationale on which to base contracting public work.

Privatization is self-enforcing. The combination of carefully written contracts and market competition will, it was argued, result in a natural process of enforcement, a kind of public sector invisible hand.

Even a rudimentary understanding of the history of corruption in American government comes with knowledge that graft, kickbacks, skimming, and the like all have to do with contracts between governments and private or nonprofit organizations. Have we forgotten the HUD scandal? Have we forgotten the Ill Winds defense purchasing scandal and all of the smaller local scandals associated with contract transactions? Privatization increases the number and range of contracts and thereby the number and range of possible ethical lapses. In the light

94

of increased contracting are governments strengthening their contract management capabilities, a point made by everyone who has looked seriously at contracting? The Department of Defense is one of the few examples of large-scale training and preparation for increased contracting.

Sclar's research shows both that contracts are not self-enforcing and that governments are not doing a good job of preparing themselves to manage contracts. Sclar reminds us that, "a self-enforcing and competitively renewable contract to perform work for the public sector is similar to the perfectly competitive market—an ideal. The reality of public work is that much of it is complex to perform, complex to administer and complex to evaluate." Because of the problems of accountability and potential corruption associated with contracting, even with an investment in good contract management, the evidence indicates that problems of accountability and control persist. "This does not auger well for calls to privatize larger, more complex, and less easily evaluated services such as public safety, education, corrections, health, human services, and welfare, although these services comprise the bulk of the public budget."

Lest this treatment of privatization and government contracting seem relentlessly negative, let me turn to the good news and to Sclar's informed wisdom on the subject.

First, for a very long time there have been good government contracts. Sclar indicates that carefully specified services or deliverables are key, such as all of the minute details that go into a contract to build a public building or repair a mile of road. The results of such a contract are precise, clear, and measurable. As contracts move from the tangible to the intangible, precision and careful specification become more difficult, as in the case of job training for persons about to lose welfare benefits, or cancer research. Sclar also recommends agreed-upon cost accounting formats, which facilitate tracking contract compliance and effectiveness.

Second, attempting through government to create a market seldom works. If there is not a market for a public good it is probably because there is no demonstrable way to make money on the service or to solve the free rider problem.

Third, rather than a competitive market, the best privatizing/contracting systems do not emulate the market and are in fact the antithesis of the market. Sclar describes them as "relational contracts," contracts which include systems for improving direct government service provision by having "contracts" between government and its subdivisions such as police, fire protection, social services—a model developed famously in Indianapolis. And relational contracts include the maintenance and improvement of contracts between governments and essentially sole providers, using a form of network theory and the logic of what has come to be called governance. Governance does not distinguish between public and private in the traditional way, but instead defines as public all things done at taxpayer expense by whatever form of institution does them. Therefore, when a contract is struck, the institution receiving the contract—Boeing, RAND Corporation, Catholic Charities—become essentially public, taking on partnerships with their contractors. Sclar calls for the development and improvement of this model, both on the government side by investing further in contract management and accounting systems, and the contracting side by developing a public service ethic.

Paul Light and Donald Kettl make the same argument.

Finally, based on his findings, Sclar sets out seven rules for improving both privatization and the public sector:

1. Carefully delineate the output of any public service considered for reorganizing by contract.
2. Get the accounting right.
3. Compare in-house providers and external providers.
4. Fully address contract transaction costs.
5. Recognize that public contracting is different from private contracting.
6. Compare three things—direct service, ordinary contracting, and relational contracting.
7. Make meaningful employee participation possible.
8. Get politics out of contracting.

Dismantling Democratic States

It sometimes happens that the most unique and interesting perspective on a subject comes indirectly, on a tangent, and so it is with the best book on public administration I have read in the last year, Ezra Suleiman's brilliant *Dismantling Democratic States*. Suleiman, very well known in the study of comparative politics, brings to the study of public administration and particularly bureaucracy, a fresh and exciting perspective. As a comparativist, he finds patterns and connections and puts them together, and the public administration patterns he finds are, put mildly, disturbing.

Suleiman argues that government effectiveness in France, Germany, Spain, the United Kingdom, and the United States gradually is being dismantled from within. All five countries are so-called mature democracies, their maturity based in part on the development and maintenance of merit-based and professionalized civil service systems. Indeed, according to Suleiman, a merit-based professional bureaucracy is essential to the development and continuation of democratic government. "It is not an accident that modern mass democracy and the development of what came to be recognized as the modern bureaucracy went hand-in-hand. The modern democratic state was built upon the bureaucratic structure that undergirds this state. Political leaders of the emerging democratic states from the early nineteenth century to the late twentieth century recognized that whatever the goals of the state—controlling a vast empire, creating an educational system, guaranteeing democratic procedures, conducting war, establishing the welfare state, collecting taxes—each necessitates a highly organized, basically nonpolitical instrument at its disposal."

"Why," he asks, "at this point in history, has a reform movement arisen championing the gradual dismantling of bureaucracy?... In almost all democratic societies we have witnessed over the past two decades an incontestable phenomenon: relentless attacks on and denigration of the state. The public sector as a whole and the state's chief instrument—the bureaucracy—have borne the brunt of the merciless attacks. This is true of societies, like the United States, that have always exhibited a profound mistrust of state authority as it is of societies that have historically attributed a sacrosanct status to their state."

Bureaucratic reform, marching under several banners—reinventing government, new public management, managerialism, political responsiveness, performance management—is systematically dismantling state administrative capacity. These common features of bureaucratic reform are found in many mature democratic states: Elected officials run as much against bureaucracy and the state as they run against their political opponents; systems of sustained incumbency and high level patronage come to characterize the political and electoral institutions of the state; issues of management take on increased salience in the political and electoral institutions of the state as matters of policy are rendered banal; systems of contracting-out and privatization hollow-out the administrative institutions of the state; upper echelons of merit-based civil service are being replaced by a cadre of political appointees; and state bureaucracy is thought to be primarily in service to the party in power rather than in service to the state or to the public interest.

Has bureaucratic reform made democratic states more effective or more legitimate in the eyes of their citizens? Suleiman answers this question with a resounding "No!" In fact, it is bureaucratic reform, thus conceived, that is dismantling the democratic state.

"All-out politicization is usually defended on the grounds that it makes executives more effective.... Reagan may have succeeded very well in controlling the bureaucracy and the literature of rational choice analysts overflows with hero-worship bordering on idolatry.... Yet no calculation seems to have been made of the costs of Reagan's actions in terms of future effectiveness or on the adverse effects on the competence of the bureaucracy. I know of no analysis that convincingly demonstrates that the drive of one chief executive to politicize the bureaucracy has successfully improved the responsiveness and efficiency of this institution for his successors.

"In the end, the attacks on the federal government ... achieve none of the grandiose goals of reducing alienation, creating a sense of community, increasing participation, or increasing trust in government. These noble objectives are merely invoked to justify the reduction in the role of government. Clinton and Gore learned that politicians who live by denigrating the functions they were elected to perform end up denigrating politics, public service, and the functions they assume.... There is simply no evidence that reducing a central government's functions increases people's trust in government or people's trust in one another. In fact, the opposite may well be the case.... [B]y attacking the very functions they are elected to carry out, politicians have increased alienation from politics and mistrust of politics and political institutions.

"If interest groups associated with the party in power have an open door to the bureaucracy, as is more and more the case, how are citizens expected to trust their elected leaders? Cutting waste is not what elicits the trust of political leaders and political institutions. It has become a means by which politicians distract attention from the increasingly politicized way of governing.... [T]he absence of a professional bureaucracy may offer short-term benefits to governments, but it also renders governments less able to carry out their duties. If democratic states cannot act effectively, democracy is inevitably fragilized.

"[A]fter the initial gratitude shown to the heroes of September 11, 2001—fireman, police, public officials of all sorts, in short, all public servants—the importance accorded public institutions diminished very sharply. Indeed, it was as if the fight against terrorism could not be entrusted to the state's own institutions and servants. President Bush's current plan, as shown in the creation of the Department of Homeland Security, is nothing less than the privatization of the federal government. The 170,000 employees of the newly created department will not receive civil service protection. In addition, more than half of the federal employees (some 85,000) will become employees of private contractors. Democratic societies are based on legitimacy, which itself is largely based on effectiveness. How can governments preserve their legitimacy if they deny themselves the means of being effective?

"[E]ven with the inexorable trend of democracy, the state remains the main guardian of order, of security, of social harmony and a source for engendering trust. These functions no doubt require a leaner, more efficient and less costly bureaucratic apparatus. But they require an apparatus nonetheless. Trust in the professionalism of political authority—what Weber called the 'impersonal' aspect of bureaucratic authority—remain ingredients of a democratic order."

If, like me, you sometimes like to read things that stir you up, read Ezra Suleiman's splendid *Dismantling Democratic States*.

Public Administration With an Attitude

Some months ago a dear friend of many years said about this column: "It is public administration with an attitude." We laughed and then the conversation turned to other things. In the days and months since I have often thought about the phrase "public administration with an attitude" and its meaning and especially its intent. With your indulgence, this column will put to work the meaning and intent of public administration with an attitude.

Public administration is a profession, like many others, and public administration is the study of our profession and the public context in which we do our professional work. The best of public administration is, however, much more than our profession or its study; it is a state of mind, a conviction, a set of deeply held shared values. Public administration with an attitude is the forthright, unapologetic, no-punches-pulled, articulation of our state of mind and our convictions. And it is the vigorous defense of those convictions and shared values.

In the early history of modern public administration it was seldom necessary to forthrightly describe, let alone defend, our convictions or beliefs. Because the core values of our field—representative democratic government, merit appointment and promotion, efficiency, economy, equity, separation from politics, and a commitment to the greater good—were broadly assumed and accepted, we were comfortable with justifying concepts such as bureaucratic neutrality and a passion for anonymity. There was no need for an attitude.

But no longer. Ours is an era of bureaucrat bashing, political micro-management, and a government that is not the solution but the problem. It is strange that we have been so passive in this era, so stuck in the logic of an earlier time. In the main, public administration has accepted, and in some cases even embraced, downsizing, more contracting-out, privatization, and in some cases even political micro-management. We seldom speak out when it is evident to any sophomore that public administrators are being asked to effectively administer deeply flawed public policy such as the Internal Revenue Code. It has simply been more comfortable for us to go along, to make the best of bad ideas.

I submit that it is time for public administration with an attitude. Happy to say, we have several wonderful examples of public administration with an attitude.

First, consider the growing literature on public administrators with an attitude, our bureaucratic role models who have shown both courage and effectiveness. I recommend Terry Cooper and Dale Wright's excellent collection *Exemplary Public Administrators*, Robert Hought's *Giants in Management* and Mark Moore's *Creating Public Value*. These collections indicate that greatness in public administration requires an attitude of forthright advocacy of the purposes of an agency, a clear commitment to the core value of public administration, and great courage and persistence.

Second, a strong public administration with an attitude position on downsizing can be found in Paul Light's *The True Size of Government* and Vernon Dale Jones' *Downsizing the Federal Government*. These analyses indicate that downsizing cripples agencies and reduces their capacity to deliver services. Some agencies have more staff than they need, but these agencies usually have powerful political allies. It is the unpopular and vulnerable agencies that are rendered less effective by downsizing.

Third, an equally strong public administration with an attitude position on contracting-out is found in two of Don Kettl's books, *Government by Proxy: Managing Federal Programs* and *Sharing*

Power: Public Governance and Private Markets. Two particularly perceptive books by Lester Salamon, *Rethinking Public Management: Third-Party Government and the Changing Forms of Government Action* and *Beyond Privatization* are also strongly recommended. My reading of these analyses concludes that contracting-out seldom produces real competition, often diminishes public control of outcomes, often disperses responsibility, usually reduces government capacity and institutional memory, and to top it off, only rarely actually saves money. When contracting-out does save money it is almost always on the basis of either lower wages or fewer workers. Practicing public administration with an attitude should at a minimum suggest that we present these arguments and findings to those who can only see what they imagine to be the benefits of contracting-out.

Fourth, it is fashionable in public administration to embrace reform, reengineering, reinvention. Public administration with an attitude would be represented by George Downs and Patrick Larkey's wonderful book *The Search for Government Efficiency: From Hubris to Hopelessness* and Paul Light's equally good *The Tides of Reform.* These analyses describe "reform fatigue" as well as the over-blown promises and weak results of reform.

Fifth, what should the public administrator do when faced with the dilemma of administering an agency with deeply flawed policy? My favorite public administration with an attitude sources are John Rohr's *Public Service, Ethics and Constitutional Practice*, Terry Cooper's *The Responsible Administrator*, James Bowman's Ethical *Frontiers in Public Management*, and Deborah Stone's brilliant *Policy Paradox and Political Reason.*

Sixth, one enduring problem of public administration is the management of agencies dealing with difficult social problems—schooling, drug abuse, gangs, prisons, poverty. It is fashionable to be critical of schools and their management, of the police as they attempt to enforce the drug laws, and so forth. The best public administration with an attitude source on this problem is Erwin Hargrove and John Glidewell's *Impossible Jobs in Public Management.* They demonstrate that the challenge is the intractable nature of some social problems and ordinarily not the quality of the management of impossible jobs.

Finally, the best overall public administration with an attitude sources are Charles Goodsell's wonderful *A Case For Bureaucracy: A Public Administration Polemic* and Joel Handler's especially thoughtful *Down From Bureaucracy: The Ambiguity of Privatization and Empowerment.*

The perceptive reader might fairly argue that public administration with an attitude is merely a defense of the status quo and of all bureaucrats. On the contrary. Public administration with an attitude argues that most public sector problems trace not to poor management but to flawed policy, political interference, inadequate resources, impossible jobs, and over-blown reforms. Public administration with an attitude simply calls it as it is.

Public Organizations, Management, and Innovation

There are two rather distinct approaches to the subject. The first is the managed innovation approach favored particularly in business, including contemporary innovation ideas such as best practices and benchmarking. This approach is influenced by awards (The Baldridge, the Harvard Innovation, etc.) and rankings, and by management consultants. Managed innovation is primarily informed by repeated and generally uncritical narratives of the successful use of innovations, which get called best practices, and are carried forward to other organizations in a diffusion of innovation. The second approach is sustained innovation, an approach identified particularly with governmental and nonprofit organizations. The sustaining innovation model is informed by the splendid research of Paul C. Light in the recent book *Sustaining Innovation: Creating Nonprofit and Governmental Organizations that Innovate Naturally.* Light bases his findings on in-depth studies of 28 institutions that have endured, survived, and innovated all along the way.

A comparison of the two models appears below.

Virtually all descriptions of organizing or reorganizing for best practice-benchmarking are expressed in terms of systems of management, control, and delegated authority. There is little evidence of the application of managed innovation logic resulting in decentralization and greater work group autonomy. Innovation research however, indicates that innovations are more likely in flexible, loosely coupled institutional (or non-institutional) settings.

It is the case that particularly creative persons with breakthrough ideas start organizations—Steve Jobs at Apple, Bill Gates at Microsoft—and become the heroic leaders in innovation narratives. The problem, of course, is sustaining a momentum of not only the quality production of the innovative product, but the development of new innovative products. Organizations in the public and nonprofit sectors almost always receive a new leader rather than the energy of a creative leader. The Department of Agriculture, the State of Kansas, or the Ford Foundation are not phased out to be replaced by new organizations led by creative leaders. So, as we say in politics and public management, "Ya dance with who brung ya."

Johan P. Olsen in his book *Administration Reform and Theories of Organization*, however, describes leadership as:

"[T]he institution is a political and moral order, a collection of long-lasting standard operating procedures—reflecting values, principles, and beliefs that are shared. The primary task of the leader is to guarantee enough order and autonomy to enable the pursuit of collective purposes. Leaders are 'gardeners'—they support rather than direct. They are obligated to defend uniform and collective standards of appropriateness, with reference to what is best for the institution."

It should not be assumed however, that there are not great leaders in government and nonprofit institutions, because there are. These great leaders, however, as the best research on public leadership finds, are more like gardeners than high profile visionary heroes.

No popular phrase better describes the modern conception of responsibility than Al Davis' now famous, "just win, baby." It is the bottom line that matters most. In our time the bottom line is summed each quarter, each month, each day. Searching elsewhere for best practices and applying them through benchmarking is a bit like catching the next good wave in the innovation surf.

Strategic planning logic—clarify goals, choose the most important among them, fix on one or two goals which best represents the institutions core purpose, set up measures of how the institution will know how well it is achieving these goals, look at other institutions to find their best practices and import the best, and use benchmarks—is at the heart of the managed innovation model. It is an organizational adaptation of stimulus-response, means and ends, and logical positivist rationality. Based on empirical observation, scholars and researchers long ago modified and softened this model with the logic of muddling through and buffered rationality. The common empirically tested model is described in formal terms as successive limited comparisons and is compared with the rational-comprehensive model, which has virtually no empirical warrant.

A certain level of goal ambiguity leaves wiggle room, invites possibilities and generally opens things up. Techniques for the effective management and navigation of ambiguity are part of virtually all management textbook and courses. It is useful to remember Frederickson's Rule: Goals are deceptive—the unaimed arrow never misses.

All versions of managed innovation call for greater precision in the measurement of results. In technology this makes great sense because we want software, medicine, and machines to do what they are supposed to do. The problem is exporting this logic to the murky world of human behavior and collective action. Virtually all research on the subject indicates that the challenges of precise measurement of performance in the public and nonprofit sectors are legion. On this point I am partial to the wisdom of Sir Josiah Stamp:

"Public agencies are very keen on amassing statistics—they collect them, add them, raise them to the nth power, take the cube roots, and prepare wonderful diagrams. But what you must never forget is that every one of those figures comes in the first instance from the village watchman, who just puts down what he damn pleases."

All effective organizations must have precise revenues, expenditures, budgets and some ways to know how well they are accomplishing their purposes. But, following managed innovation assumptions, it is understood that performance measures are exactly that, measures, and that they only represent reality. They are subject to scrutiny, to debate and even to dismissal if they are nonsense. Performance measures do not answer questions; they are questions. Under conditions of sustained innovation it is far better to approximate an answer to the right question, which is often vague, than to search for the exact answer to the wrong question. Such answers can always be made more precise; they are still answers to the wrong question.

One of the fashions of the day, particularly among organizational consultants, is to call for the creation of a culture of creativity, innovation, and even invention. Leadership, it is assumed, has the capacity to mold and shape the organization so that there will be a climate of creativity, an opening of the human capacity for change and for collective improvement and breakthroughs. Thirty years ago in a wonderful little review of literature at the time, John Jawkes, in *The Sources of Invention* wrote:

"The writings on invention, whilst vast and ever increasing, are of extraordinarily mixed quality. There seems to be no subject in which traditional and uncritical stories, casual rumors, sweeping generalizations, myths and conflicting records more widely abound. No one can entirely escape the mild mesmerizing influence of the subject."

Jawkes could well have been describing current innovation fads and their consulting firm advocates, the total quality managers, the scorecard balancers, the process reengineers, the government reinventors, the best practicers, the benchmarkers and the rest of the management innovation pushers.

Years ago the Bell Laboratories tried to find the common characteristics of creative types in complex organizations. It is sad to report, they found only two: an exceptional tolerance for messy work environments and a well-developed sense of humor. What they specifically did not find was some secret formula by which managers can, by organizational means, cause there to be creativity.

The best contemporary study of the nature of organizational innovation and creativity is *Breakthroughs!* written by P. Rangamath Nayak and John P. Ketteringham. They directed a team of researchers from Arthur D. Little in a study of fourteen commercial innovations so significant and lasting as to constitute breakthroughs.

Their study included significant innovations in products, services, and industrial processes including the compact disc, the VCR, the ulcer drug Tagamet, the CAT scan, the hollow corporation (Nike), overnight airmail package service (FedEx) and, of all things, Club Med. In their study they sought a broad spectrum of products, services and industries and for this reason their findings are important to those of us interested in innovation and creativity not only in the private sector, but also in the public and nonprofit sectors.

They found that breakthroughs grew from rich organizational soil, barren organizational soil, rocky soil, or no soil at all. Breakthroughs have come from organizations that foster creativity as well as those with poor records of innovation. They have come from creative teams that were joined by their management, ignored by their management, supported only belatedly by management, misunderstood by management, and castigated by management. Breakthroughs can emerge just as readily from no organization at all.

Breakthroughs are not organizational creations, although they may be catalyzed or inhibited by organizations. But, it will not surprise the astute reader to learn that once breakthroughs are successful they are eagerly claimed by the organization and particularly by management. Breakthroughs are much more like works of art than like works of commerce or public service. Groups of people who together accomplish breakthroughs behave more like the disciples of a visionary than like the autonomous graduates of prestigious business schools or public administration programs.

The *Breakthroughs!* research team reviewed their findings in terms of myths and realities, thus:

Myth: Breakthroughs come from ideas no one ever had before.

Reality: Most breakthrough ideas are not original but are made newly applied or useful. It is not so much the originality of the idea as the relentless and single minded pursuit of the idea that results in a breakthrough.

Myth: Innovations occur through genius creators.

Reality: There are many forms of innovation—innovators who are best at the initial conception of a process or technology, innovators best at working with and guiding innovative teams, and even innovators who are essentially idea fine-tuners.

Myth: Great ideas come from little guys.

Reality: Certain innovations, especially those that require relatively small investments of capital but large commitments of individual labor, tend to come from independent entrepreneurs. But, innovations that require substantial financial investment and teamwork often emerge within big organizations.

Myth: Innovation and creativity respond to unfulfilled needs.

Reality: Some innovations are direct responses to unmet and obvious needs. But just as many innovations are ideas for which there is as yet no obvious need. It turns out that garbage can theory is right. In the decision soup churning about in the organizational garbage can, there will be problems looking for solutions, and solutions looking for problems to solve, questions looking for answers, and answers looking for questions. For example, did we need the Internet? Yes, but we didn't know it; once the Internet was available we have discovered its usefulness and now depend on it.

Myth: Innovations require a special sort of environment.

Reality: The *Breakthroughs!* research shows that happier workers are more generally productive. But a happy and productive environment does not necessarily nurture latent creativity. The idea that organizational culture can be managed or created so as to either support or stifle creativity or the innovative spirit has no evidence to support it. The astute Lawrence Lynn once wrote that "the manager who claims to be creating a culture of creativity will certainly be regarded as a pompous ass by those in the organization who are really creative."

The *Breakthroughs!* team did identify some barriers to innovation. When risk-taking and failure are punished, creativity is less likely.

Discouraging experimentation probably discourages innovation. Initial statements of creative ideas are seldom fully-formed and well-defended. Managers wishing to look smart will attack such ideas as unfamiliar, unproven, risky. Every organization has people who know all the reasons new things cannot be done.

Organizations need to be led by courageous people who know when to say yes, even at the risk of failure. It helps the creative process to put managers, researchers, and others in the upper levels of the hierarchy with clients, customers, and citizens and tries to get managers and researchers to shut-up and listen. Innovations often come from individuals and groups with a track record of innovation.

Finally, it is helpful to keep the processes of innovation and creativity at arms length from the organizational legal staff, lest they find some law or regulation against it!

I close with the wisdom of Voltaire: "The search for the best is the enemy of the good."

Book Five
Public Administration as Reform

Hijacking Public Administration

Consider this proposition: Much of public administration has been hijacked, repackaged and relabeled. Public administration is now known as "government reform." The government-reform project is based on assumptions that much of American government is ill organized, poorly managed, very costly and generally ineffective. Taken together, these assumptions are the platform for the premise that there is an organizational and managerial crisis in American government.

In a brilliant paper recently presented at a symposium on the future of the civil service by Hal Rainey and Ed Kellough and an equally brilliant article in the latest issue of the *Journal of Public Administration Research and Theory* by Hal Rainey and Paula Steinbauer, they rightly point out that government reformers must claim a crisis so they can sell their reform. Because the marketplace of ideas is crowded, one would not suggest that there is a public management "issue" or a public management "concern." No, there is a crisis. In the age of hyperbole it would not do to claim there are some problems and some pretty good solutions. Serious reform can only be justified by claiming an urgent and dire crisis.

The problem is, as Rainey and Kellough write, "The administrative branch of government in the United States is not in crisis and has not been in recent decades. Problems and shortcomings abound, and they can always be labeled crisis, but no general, severe crisis exists." The two agencies accounting for half of federal budget outlays, the Social Security Administration and the Department of Defense, are marvels of effective administration. While the effectiveness and the administration of these two agencies can always be improved, they are hardly in crisis.

The reform project prefers to deal with the crisis of public management with a now familiar series of reforms: 1) reducing regulatory controls on personnel practices, purchasing rules, and the like; 2) empowering or widening the discretion of public managers; 3) greater privatization and contracting out; 4) pay for individual performance as well as overall organizational effectiveness incentives; 5) measuring performance; 6) using competition and other market concepts to enhance performance.

These reforms and the crisis logic upon which they rest, have proved to be good executive politics as demonstrated by the popularity of the National Performance Review. They are also good legislative politics, witness the seemingly endless series of management reforms such as the Government Performance and Results Act. But the executive and legislative "tides of reform," as Paul Light puts it, have been so relentless that public managers are so busy doing the tinkering of reform that they are less an less able to manage their agencies. Public administration has thus become government reform. The reform project may be very good politics but not very good public administration.

What, then, is good public administration? Rainey and Kellough and Rainey and Steinbauer review seven studies of high performance government agencies and found several common characteristics among them.

First, they discovered that these high performance agencies are standard-brand federal offices and bureaus, using ordinary personnel, purchasing, and other systems of public administration. Put another way, they are unreformed.

Second, effective leadership is critical in high performance agencies. This leadership is characterized by stability, many leaders or teams of leaders, leaders committed to the agency mission, and leaders who are especially effective in coping with political and administrative constraints.

Third, particularly effective government agencies set up well-designed tasks and provide the technology and other resources needed to accomplish these tasks. Task design emphasizes both intrinsic motivation (desire to serve, desire to accomplish the agency's mission) and extrinsic rewards (promotions, career development, pay).

Fourth, there is lots of training in high performance public agencies. In addition, other aspects of human resource development such as effective recruitment, selection, placement, and career development are evident.

Fifth, they tend to have agency missions, which are relatively clear and have obvious "public" qualities. These agencies often have influential constituents and clients (the elderly, for example) and good relations with them. They also have effective managerial relations with partners and suppliers such as contractors and vendors. These agencies tend to enjoy favorable public opinion (eg., the Postal Service).

Sixth, high performance government agencies tend to have reasonable autonomy from political authorities. Political oversight tends to be attentive, supportive, and delegative.

Finally, these studies of high performance public organizations agree with the reform project on one matter—the empowerment of public managers.

Workers in high performance public organizations do not engage in innovation, creativity, or adaptability because there are clear-cut incentives for them to do so. When asked why they are creative, their primary reason was their wish "to do the right thing."

The primary indicators of high performance public agencies spring from the origins and traditions of public administration as well as modern applications of public administration. High performance public organizations are seldom helped by the fads of government reform, and as Paul Light indicates, are often harmed by the reform project.

Lessons from Government Reform

It is Peter Drucker's position that the application of rational market-based logic to the public sector will have serious problems if public programs are set up with overly lofty objectives, such as to improve health care, aid the disadvantaged, or make the workplace safe. But

112

broad objectives are often the essence of public policy. Business applications will also fail, he claimed, if they are applied to programs that have two or more competing purposes, such as the simultaneous punishment and rehabilitation of convicts. But in a pluralistic society public policy almost always serves multiple purposes. Business applications, he further claimed, will fail if they are non-incremental grand new ideas that need to work on the first try. Business practices applied to government will not work if the goals set out in legislation and in budgets pursuant to that legislation are vague. Finally, business applications in government will fail if the goals are high and the resources needed to reach those goals are meager.

What Drucker failed to understand is politics. Legislation is always a compromise, a compromise that usually includes competing purposes, lofty purposes, intentionally vague language, policy that needs to work on the first try, and never enough money. Drucker wanted government to be like business, then it could be managed like business. Although he may not have realized it, he was exactly right—the application of business practices to government will fail so long as government insists on acting like government. The problem, however, is not, as Drucker imagined, the management of governments. The problem is politics.

The migration of business innovations to government is a widely studied phenomenon, a field of research known as the public management reform literature. It has an honorable provenance beginning with the first application of serious bookkeeping in American government during Alexander Hamilton's service as Secretary of the Treasury.

In the past 25 years reforms have called for selling government assets (the Tennessee Valley Authority, the Grand Coulee Dam, and many others), greatly expanded contracting out (erroneously called privatization), bureaucratic downsizing and enhanced political control of administrators. All reforms are argued in terms of greater efficiency. Reinventing government is the most recent, a reform combining contracting out, risk taking to enhance the prospects for innovation, performance measurement of outcomes rather than outputs, and customer service. It has been broadly influential at all levels of American government, holding out the promise of getting more and better government for less money. In the Clinton-Gore era this resulted in an astounding 11 percent drop in the federal civilian work force. The problem is that the federal budget continued to grow, the difference being largely made up by contracting out. Paul Light's study *The True Size of Government*, demonstrates that for every one federal civilian employee there are now eight persons (actually full-time equivalent persons) who trace their income to the federal government. So, the claim that the federal government is smaller and that the era of big government is over is little more than political rhetoric. The problem with applying business principles to government as the basis for reform is well described in the best book on the subject, George W. Downs and Patrick O. Larkey's *The Search for Government Efficiency: From Hubris to Helplessness*. They conclude that:

1) Governments in the United States are much more efficient and effective than most citizens believe. Their efficiency has improved dramatically over the past 100 years and compares favorably with that of their foreign counterparts. Moreover, the efficiency of government bureaucracies is much closer to that of private-sector bureaucracies than is generally acknowledged. Substantial problems with government performance remain, however, and these problems are much harder to solve than those of the past, which were connected with widespread graft and corruption and the absence of accounting systems. The chances are slim that there will be a technical or conceptual breakthrough in improving government efficiency that will have the impact that the discovery of broad-spectrum antibiotics had on medicine or that the discovery of the transistor or microchip had on electronics. The chances are nil that the solutions to government's managerial problems already exist in the management technologies of the private sector.

2) The bulk of the improvements in government efficiency that have taken place in recent years have resulted not so much from overt, grandiose reform schemes as from a host of modest, tactical reforms. There appears to be an inverse relationship between the amount of fanfare associated with any given reform and its positive effects on govern-

ment performance. Business methods are much less appropriate to improving the efficiency and effectiveness of government than is commonly believed. The methods are not the panaceas for inefficiency and ineffectiveness in government [or business] that some believe them to be. There are intrinsic differences between the functions of government and the functions of business, and these require different managerial methods.

3) There are real limits to the efficiency and effectiveness that any government can achieve. These limits arise from the nature of the problems that governments are obligated to address, from the constraints that governments must honor in attempting to solve the problems, from the large scale of many government organizations, and from the intentionally adversarial character of government processes.

Government reform history teaches that the political character of much government inefficiency cannot be overcome through the installation of a program, a new organizational structure or a system that is ultimately controlled by the same people who have incentives to protect values other than efficiency.

Some Thoughts on Reform

I recently participated in a two-day conference on government reform that focused particularly on the implementation of the Government Performance and Results Act (GPRA) of 1993. The presenters include G. Edward DeSeve, the acting deputy director for management at the Office of Management and Budget, who is leading the overall government implementation of GPRA, and David M. Walker, the comptroller general. In addition there were several presentations by the leading implementers of GPRA in the cabinet departments. Having listened to their talk, watched the obligatory Powerpoint presentations, and read their reports, here are some observations.

First, one must be impressed with the good will, creativity, energy, and sheer bureaucratic determination shown in the implementation of

GPRA and the Performance Assessment Rating Tool (PART) as well as other recent reforms. In the face of daunting problems associated with issues of goal conflict and ambiguity and the details of performance measurement, all bureaus, agencies and offices have prepared strategic plans spelling out goals and objectives and the means by which these goals and objectives will be measured. These offices and bureaus also formulated plans for linking the measurement of performance to their budget submissions, as called for in the law. Despite what must be serious reservations about measuring performance in disciplines such as foreign affairs, the bureaucracy will make GPRA and PART happen.

Second, it is increasingly evident that what Paul Light describes as the "hurricanes of reform" are taking their toll. He writes that reform hurricanes "blow through Washington with what seems to be increasing frequency, and, dare one suggest, damage." Reform efforts (the National Performance Review, the Government Management Reform Act, etc.) have piled on reforms to the point that management has become reform. The combination of downsized staff and piled up reforms has shifted management resources away from management toward reform, as if the two were the same thing.

We may be moving to the paradox of federal agencies being less well managed while at the same time their performance is much better measured.

Third, under conditions of political gridlock, it is increasingly evident that our governmental leaders are less and less able to decide *what* to do and are, therefore, much more interested in *how* to do things. Among the political classes we seem to have fewer law and policy makers and more management reformers with a better way.

Fourth, performance reforms have changed the language of government. For example, USAID grants are now "results packages." Each element of USAID grants are "strategic objectives." Progress is defined in terms of "quarterly reports of results indicators." The language is strewn with "governance," "partners," "donors," "performance teams," (what we used to call departments) and so forth. As management becomes reform, the language of management is likewise reformed to become a language of reform.

Finally, even when administration is at its best, much of it is routine, predictable, orderly, and organized. In many ways top quality administration is so good that it is unnoticed, ordinary. Things just get done and get done well. David Mathews, in his wisdom, suggests that the best in democratic government can be found in doing the ordinary a bit differently, rather than doing something different from the ordinary. When management reform is approached as doing something entirely different, with attendant overpromising and overapplying, it loses its potential to enhance agency effectiveness.

In the end, as Paul Light so wisely points out, the country is making much more progress on management reform than it is making on election reform or on controlling the influence of interest groups. At this time what we appear to need most is political rather than management reform.

Real Reform

In the same way that events tend to concentrate the mind, events focus public institutions on their core purposes. The events of September 11, 2001, and the challenge of global terrorism helps us, as Dwight Waldo was fond of saying, "see things in the entire." Although certainly no Waldo, I shall attempt here to see things in the entire by considering several of the subjects that have dominated public administration over the past two decades.

The reform hegemony has dominated public administration for the last two decades, everyone seemed to agree that things simply had to be changed. "Re" words were everywhere—reform, reinvent, reengineer, results. If you rejected the consensus that our public institutions were broken and needed to be fixed you were a retrograde (another "re" word) dolt blindly defending the status quo. Reform has been piled on reform to the point of reform fatigue. Downsizing has resulted in fewer staff. The rush to contract-out has resulted in a sharply diminished capacity to manage contracts. Worst of all, in much of the rhetorical justification for public sector reforms, the reformers have characterized public employees as hopeless bureaucrats and their agencies and jurisdictions as unresponsive and wasteful.

Then came September 11, 2001, and now we understand. When our country, our states, or our cities are threatened, we value order, predictability and reliability and we expect our public institutions to provide the security that comes from order, predictability, and reliability. On one hand, our air travel security system badly failed that test. On the other hand, local fire, police, and emergency services passed the test with remarkable competence and unsurpassed courage.

Consider the differences. Local police and fire are distinctly public, governmental, and concentrated. They are, in the language of organizational theorists, high culture organizations, with extensive training, uniforms, rank, ceremonies, and deep traditions. They are unionized and demand fair pay and benefits. They are loyal to one another and to their city, a kind of old-fashioned reciprocity, which exchanges dedication and hard work for fair pay and respect. Far from perfect (we all know the challenges of police corruption and the problems of race in the police and fire services), when called upon for effective service and heroic tasks, they do not hesitate. The close connection between the New York City police and fire services and Mayor Guiliani are well known and serve as an interesting example of loyalty and reciprocity, including both its positive and negative characteristics.

By comparison, the air travel security system is highly fragmented and anything but concentrated. The airlines are expected to provide well-maintained airplanes and reliable, safe services, they are also expected to guarantee that passengers will be safe from other passengers. They attempted to do this through a series of contracts and subcontracts that like most contracting regimes, emphasized cost savings at the expense of competence. Linkages between the federalized air traffic control system (until recently there were calls to contract-out air traffic control), local government airport authorities and departments, airlines, the Federal Aviation Administration (FAA), and the Department of

Transportation (DoT), are complex and fragmented. But, in the logic of high reliability systems, such systems can work if there is very tight coupling between the parts, including high levels of training, low staff turnover, contingency drills and exercises, and, above all, the financial resources needed to do the job. Some parts of the system, such as air traffic control and airline pilots and staff, could be described as high culture organizations practicing tight coupling. But other parts of the air travel security system, particularly passenger and baggage screening, are the opposite of high culture organizations and are very loosely coupled.

The events of September 11, 2001, put the differences between local police and fire services and the air travel safety system in bold relief. Running counter to both the political and the public administration hegemonies of the last two decades, the Congress responded by federalizing the processes of passenger and baggage screening. In time we will see a high culture uniformed, trained, fairly paid cadre of public servants to vouchsafe our air travel. Congressman DeLay, who opposed federalizing air passenger and baggage screening on the grounds that it may be harder to fire public employees, was right. In return for a highly trained, low-turnover, reliable cadre of air safety public servants, we must provide job security. How can we possibly expect them to be loyal to us if we are not loyal to them?

Easily the clearest thinking on this subject, thinking decidedly counter to the reigning hegemony, can be found in Larry Terry's splendid book *Leadership of Public Bureaucracies*. Terry argues that what really matters is public institutional integrity—patterns of distinct competencies and shared value commitments. In somewhat more elaborate terms he describes institutional integrity as the "completeness, wholeness, soundness, and persistence of administrative processes, value commitments, and unifying principles that determine an institution's distinctive competence." To make institutional integrity happen, leaders need power and authority and the skills to conserve the distinctive capacities of agencies, bureaus, and jurisdictions. What institutions do not need is powerful, swaggering, heroic leaders, entrepreneurs, risk-takers, and change agents. Instead public institutions need leaders who understand the institutions' core values and competencies, respect and protect their traditions, and who know how to adapt the institutions' values, competencies and traditions to new and changing circumstances. The key word here is "adapt." James Q. Wilson describes the process of institutional leadership as managing the fine-tuning and adaptive process as "added on to existing tasks without changing core tasks." Johan P. Olsen describes the public sector leader as a gardener, an anti-hero who understands the soil, the seasons, the need for careful planning and preparation, and understands deeply that ultimate productivity will be determined by careful tending and nurturing. Gardeners know institutional integrity.

The events of September 11, 2001, seen in the entire, teach us that we need a highly reliable air travel security system that is governmental, built on the logic of institutional integrity, and led by a group of very good gardeners. Fly well and safely my friends.

A Brief Essay on the Grotesque Excesses of California School Reform

Consider the wisdom of Samuel Taylor Coleridge: Every reform, however necessary, will by weak minds be carried to an excess, that itself will need reforming.

The so-called accountability features of California school reform have reached the point of such grotesque excess as to cry out for reform. More than 430,000 tenth grade students recently took the California High School Exit Examination. The results were announced and they were not good; over half of the students failed, most of them for the second time. Unless something is done, tens of thousands of students will not be able to attend a California public college or university, even if they earn good grades in high school, take the right courses, and do well on the SAT.

The demographics of those who passed and those who failed are sadly familiar. Statewide, 72 percent of the African-Americans and 70 percent of the Latinos failed. At Crenshaw High School, in one of the poorest sections of Los Angeles, only 20 percent of the class of 2004 passed the math portion of the Exit Examination and 47 percent passed the language arts portion. By comparison, 95 percent of the class of 2004 at Beverly Hills High School passed the math portion and 100 percent passed the language arts portion. These demographic patterns repeat themselves all across California, exhibiting an almost perfect correlation between income levels and test-passing effectiveness.

It is not just demographics that accounts for variations in failure or passage of the California High School Exit Examination.

- At high schools where the passage of the math portion of the test falls in the bottom 10 percent in California, 24 percent of the teachers are, on average, without full certification. In the top 25 percent of high schools with math test success, only eight percent of the teachers are, on average, lacking credentials.

- In California, minority students are five times more likely than non-minority students to have under-qualified teachers.

- Schools with a shortage of qualified teachers are also the most likely to have the worst shortages of textbooks, teaching materials, and classroom aids.

- Patterns of school overcrowding in California are also associated with demographics. The most common answer to school overcrowding is the adoption of multitrack, year-round instructional schedules. This herky-jerky schedule involves the loss of 17 days of instruction, time that is presumably made up by longer days. A highly disproportionate percentage of minority and low-income students attend multitrack schools. The average exit examination passing rate in math at multitrack year-round schools is 31 percent, while the rate of students on the standard academic year is 58 percent.

In the late 1980s and early 1990s the political leaders in California, like the political leaders in many other states, were convinced that the public schools were broken and needed fixing. Among the fashionable ways to presume to fix the public schools was to demand accountability. Individual teachers were to be accountable, entire schools and school districts were to be accountable, and, above all, students were to be accountable. In the social and political world the idea of accountability has great cachet and is very difficult to argue against. Unfortunately, accountability is also very difficult to make operational. The problem of operationalizing educational accountability was thought to be solved by the wholesale adoption of testing. Indeed in the modern world of public schooling, the word "accountability" is now generally understood to mean testing. Once universal testing was adopted in California and elsewhere, it was so easy to simply draw a line that determines who passes and who fails. Test scores have become the measure of school and student performance, the intricate calibration of academic results and, most important, the key determinant of the life prospects of many students. If a student gets, say, a 64, he or she fails. If another student gets a 65 he or she passes. Is this a reasoned basis to determine which students will be able to graduate and go on to college?

Because of the application of this logic, California has backed itself into a corner. Having gone through the same process of accountability and performance reasoning, the schools of Texas backed themselves into a similar corner in the mid-1990s. They got out of the corner by lowering the bar to the point that now almost all who take the graduate exit exam in Texas pass.

Texas, Missouri, and other states that have attempted to achieve public school accountability through the use of comprehensive graduate exit examination processes have had to either lower the bar or back away from the idea altogether. Because of this, the focus of school reform changed from whether John or Sally pass to whether the Washington School or the Lincoln School is effective. Put another way, students do not pass or fail, schools pass or fail. Now teachers are being tested, their continuation determined by how well they test. Merit pay for teachers is tied to how well their students do. Principals and superintendents are evaluated on the basis of the average test scores of students in their schools. In Missouri, the St. Louis and Kansas City School Districts (the districts with the highest percentages of minorities) are being threatened with disaccreditation. So, instead of achieving accountability by failing students, Missouri is presuming to achieve accountability by failing whole school districts. The point is the same, however, because it is either the poor and minority students who fail or the schools of the poor and minority students that fail.

At the center of this problem is the near universal belief among political leaders that the application of the accountability logic of testing constitutes school reform. To embrace accountability is to attempt school reform on the cheap. Schools are expensive and schools for the poor and disadvantaged are especially expensive. In the political world it is easy to claim that testing will bring about serious educational reform. Such a claim has the appearance of reform without having to make the hard decisions that adequately fund the public schools. There is no doubt that some schools need to be reformed, but the excesses of testing and accountability are not only not helping reform, they are hurting school children and their teachers. Every reform, as Coleridge said, will by weak minds be carried to an excess, that itself will need reforming. School reform in California has reached that point.

Measuring Performance in Theory and Practice

B ack in the 20th century the measurement of government performance was big, so big in fact it was made a law. This law, the Government Performance and Results Act of 1993 (GPRA), instructs federal agencies to develop strategic plans that include broad goals and objectives, descriptions of how these goals and objectives are to be met, and measures to be used to determine how well the goals are being met. Each agency is to annually develop a performance plan that defines the level of performance to be achieved that year for each budgeted agency program. Finally, each agency is to prepare an annual program performance report that compares actual to planned performance, a report which can be used to improve management practices, congressional decision making, and budget decisions.

GPRA caps a century of the tides of reform, to borrow Paul Light's phrase. All were designed in the hope of making government more objective, rational, and effective. And all assumed that measuring performance is essential to greater objectivity, rationality, and effectiveness. GPRA is somewhat unusual when compared with earlier reforms, because it is more comprehensive and because its origins are as much legislative as they are executive. Earlier performance measurement reforms were usually based on presidential commissions or other executive initiatives that assumed governmental effectiveness is mostly an executive or managerial matter—a tacit acceptance of the policy-administration dichotomy. We are now, however, in an era of much more direct legislative involvement in matters of administration, what Robert Gilmour and Alexis Halley call co-management and David Rosenbloom calls a legislative-centered public administration. GPRA is rather solid evidence that the legislature is full tilt into public administration and that the dichotomy is dead.

Congress ordinarily acts by making laws—in this case GPRA, a law that assumes it is possible to legislate improved government performance. GPRA was passed to further several laudable purposes: to improve confidence in government, to focus on results and service quality, to measure the effectiveness of government programs, to stimulate reforms, to improve internal management, and to improve legislative programmatic and budgetary decision making. This is the theory.

We are now 21st century public administrators with a few years of GPRA experience under our belts. At least in an initial way we are able to consider GPRA progress, prospects, and problems to GPRA in theory and GPRA in practice.

The Impact Aid program of the U.S. Department of Education will serve as a good example of GPRA in theory and practice. Originally passed in 1950 to help with the funding problems of certain school districts near federal military installations—swamped with children from military bases and without property tax support because of federal land ownership—Impact Aid has been expanded over the years. The children of both military and civilian families on or near federal facilities, children who reside on Indian lands or live in federal low-rent housing, and certain disabled children are now included. With a budget of over $900 million, the program now aids over 1,500 districts that have a minimum of 3 percent of their students—or at least 400 students—who are associated with activities of the federal government. Aid goes directly to school districts and does not pass through state education bureaucracies. Successive administrations have unsuccessfully attempted to reduce Impact Aid funding. Combining two congressionally desirable qualities—support for local education and money going to schools in many congressional districts—the Impact Aid program has become a great legislative favorite.

In their GPRA strategic plan, the Impact Aid program sets as its overall goal the provision of appropriate financial assistance for federally connected children who present a genuine burden to their school districts. To achieve this goal the program adopted these specific objectives: (1) to make payments in a timely manner; (2) to improve consultation between school districts and the Indian community to support the education of Indian children; (3) to make accurate requests; (4) to continue to maintain, repair, renovate, and transfer school facilities; (5) to improve the quality of public school facilities used to educate Indian children. Strategies were developed for meeting these objectives, as were precise measures of performance for each. The first results are in, and the Impact Aid program is generally meeting its objectives.

With this background, we return to the general issue of performance measurement in theory and practice and to the specific application of GPRA as a means of measuring performance and results in government. The table below will be used to guide this discussion

In theory, measures of performance are thought to be the answers to questions. In practice, performance measures are often themselves questions, or at least they raise as many questions as they answer. Performance measures are exactly that, quantitative representations of some reality. Because performance measures are presented quantitatively, they have the appearance of fact and convey impressions of objectivity and neutrality. In practice, such measures are quantitative interpretations of reality in exactly the same way words are narrative interpreta-tions of reality. In practice, very little is judged to be neutral and objec-tive; all performance measures may be used as arguments and weapons in policy debates. If one supports a program and performance measures appear to indicate that the program is doing well, then those perform-ance measures are seen to be objective, factual, and neutral determina-tions of program results. The same performance measures viewed by an individual or a group opposing a program will be judged to be slanted

Measuring Performance

	In Theory	In Practice
Measures of performance are:	answers objective neutral interpretations arguments	facts evidence slanted questions weapons
Results are:	aggregated for everyone	for some but not others
Performance is:	long term	short term
Policy is moved by:	data and analysis	rhetoric
What to measure:	the important	the measurable
Program domain:	comparable	particular
Causal assertion can be:	demonstrated	unclear
This program:	performs poorly	performs poorly, but things would be worse without it

interpretations of questionable data.   Officials of the Department of Education understand this, and as the descriptions of the goals, objectives, and performance measures chosen to evaluate the Impact Aid program demonstrate, they have developed a GPRA approach that recognizes the powerful political support for the program and at the same time measures performance.

One might reasonably ask: Why not measure the two rather obvious purposes of the Impact Aid program—offsetting the reduced revenues and additional costs of educating children due to federal installations, and actual educational outcomes?   The answer is that school finance issues in the 50 states and their school districts are famously complicated, so complicated that it would be expensive and time consuming to attempt to determine what actual "appropriate financial support" to federally impacted school districts should be. So, that important question is begged. So too is the question of the effects of Impact Aid on student performance. Why? Because such measures are difficult and subject to controversy and criticism, and because even if such measures were easy they would very likely yield numbers that reflect unfavorably on the program.   Such an outcome would probably not be seen as desirable on Capitol Hill or in the Department of Education. Because this is understood in practice, Impact Aid goals and objectives and their attendant performance measures are, in fact, efficiency or management goals and objectives rather than program goals and objectives.   Providing appropriate financial assistance, getting accurate checks out on time, and fixing the buildings in a timely and efficient way are management objectives. They measure the measurable and they answer questions that reflect favorably on the program while they avoid questions that are difficult and expensive to answer and which, if answered, would almost certainly anger political and administrative leaders. Put another way, the Impact Aid approach to GPRA assumes that Congress, not the Department of Education, should determine what appropriate financial assistance to federally impacted school districts ought to be. GPRA measures will, instead, tell Congress how well the Impact Aid program is being managed and leave the policy heavy lifting in Congress where it belongs. The dichotomy may not be dead after all.

Choosing to measure the measurable rather than the important in the Impact Aid program supports a theoretical point made 50 years ago by Herbert Simon. It is rational, he claimed, for administrators to use tested techniques, affordable techniques, and techniques that are near at hand. Simon also reminded us that there may be cases of generalized efficiency but there are many more cases of targeted efficiency. To ask if the Impact Aid program is efficient may be the wrong question. The right question would be: For whom is the Impact Aid program efficient? The obvious answers are, Impact Aid is particularly efficient for the school districts receiving the aid, and for the members of Congress passing it out.

There is a kind of face validity to the initial purposes of the Impact Aid program even though it may be impossible to numerically represent that validity. What would school districts swamped with federally connected children do without that aid? Even if it could be numerically demonstrated that Impact Aid was performing poorly, it could and would be argued that things would be worse in impacted districts without it. As Beryl Radin in a recent study of GPRA astutely observes, policy is influenced more by rhetoric, arguments, passions, and instincts toward fairness than by measures of performance.

Relatively non-controversial unambiguous federal programs such as the work of the Social Security Administration and the Postal Service, lend themselves to GPRA performance measurement. And they tend to be doing well. But, many government programs have little basis for reasonable comparison. The work of diplomacy, national defense, medical research, and justice are not easy to measure against business practices. In the absence of a basis of comparison, the question changes from "How well is Impact Aid doing?" to "How well are we doing Impact Aid?" In the theory of performance measurement this may be disappointing. In practice, however, it has its own rationality.

That GPRA is not achieving all that performance measurement theory would want may be disappointing to some. But on the positive side, GPRA has caused all federal agencies to carefully reconsider their purposes and to work on ways to determine (as best they can given vague and competing statutory purposes, political realities, and scarce management resource) how to measure those purposes. With these measures they will improve the quality of federal program management. The management level federal workforce has, with only a few exceptions, done a remarkable job of responding with determination and creativity to the passage of GPRA. It is public administration that is very capably bringing GPRA theory to practice.

Getting to Green

What shall we make of the Bush administration's management and program evaluation scorecards? Each new administration has its own management reform approach. President Carter applied zero-based budgeting, President Reagan appointed the Grace Commission and favored the privatization recommendations in their report, and President Clinton brought reinventing government with Vice President Gore's National Performance Review. And President Clinton's administration cooperated with Congress in the passage of the Government Performance and Results Act of 1993. In the face of the relentless tides of reform, a certain reserved enthusiasm on the part of the federal bureaucracy, the media, and the rest of the permanent government toward the Bush administration's scorecard approach is easy to understand. One of the most obvious characteristics of seasoned, jaded, and often cynical Washington insiders is their claim to have seen it all before. Let me gently suggest that Washington insiders may have seen many things before, but they have not seen the systematic application of the scorecarding approach to federal programs before. For the following reasons, the Bush administration's scorecarding approach to the management of federal programs and to overall program evaluation is deserving of thoughtful consideration.

First, there are two scorecards, one for management and one for the evaluation of the general performance of each federal agency.

Management and program evaluation have been uncoupled for the simple reason that a program may be well managed, but its accomplishments may no longer be needed, it may be unfair in the distribution of its services, or it may be extravagant. There is no question that good management is a prerequisite to agency performance and that the two are linked. On one hand, the requisites and qualities of good management are generally understood and agreed upon, and therefore the evaluation of agencies on the basis of the quality of their management can be fairly straightforward. On the other hand, the evaluation of the performance of a particular federal program (say, for example, a crop subsidy programs of the Department of Agriculture) depends on whether one favors or opposes the purposes of that program. Therefore, for purposes of scorecarding, the uncoupling of management and overall program performance makes some sense.

Second, the management scorecard format is based on relatively detailed criteria in each of five aspects of management—human capital, information technology or e-government, financial management, integration of agency performance and budget requests, and competitive sourcing. Of these, only competitive sourcing is controversial in public management circles. In the run-up to the preparation of annual executive budgets, agencies are informed of the detailed criteria in each of these five aspects of management and, over time, what would be expected of them to get a good score. The criteria, if not quantifiable, were, it is claimed, at least verifiable. As is the case in virtually all scorecarding systems, the Executive Branch Management Scorecard used a very simplistic color coding logic—red, yellow, and green. To reduce a subject as complex as the evaluation of the quality of the management of big federal programs to red, yellow, and green certainly does open the door to the criticism of vast oversimplification. But we live in a postmodern world of sound bites and fierce competition for public attention. When the first Executive Branch Management Report Card was issued, it did, at least for a time, shine a very bright light on the comparative quality of federal program management. Unfortunately that light was, in almost all cases, red. For example, Education, Energy, HUD, Interior, Justice, NSF, and even OMB, who did the evaluations, got straight reds.

Third, it might reasonably be asked if this generally negative evaluation of the quality of federal program management by the Bush administration is merely another form of bureaucrat bashing? Certainly those faithful federal public servants who have been bashed-about over the years might have good reason to see red. Nevertheless, virtually every objective analysis of federal management in recent years, such as the Volker Commission, has come to the same conclusion—after years of neglect, downsizing, political criticism, political meddling, and a cynical public, federal program management is in big trouble.

Fourth, the scorecarding reform is being done by the Office of Management and Budget. Unlike the National Performance Review lodged in Vice President Gore's office, the scorecarding reform puts the M back into OMB where (at least in most public administration circles with which I am familiar) it belongs.

Fifth, the OMB scorecarding approach attempts to tie together the logic of performance measurement and management criteria. If this is carefully done it should move the subject of management beyond grandstanding examples of bad management, such as the famous $4,000 toilet or the broken ashtray and in the direction of systematic data gathering and somewhat more objective evaluations of the essential aspects of management.

Like all proposed government management reforms, long-term success depends on follow-through. In a particularly thoughtful review and synthesis of research on the subject, Edward T. Jennings, Jr., and Meg Patrick Haist ask this question: Does performance measurement perform? Their findings can be directly applied to the question of whether the Bush administration's attempt to tie together performance measurement and the quality of federal program management by the use of scorecards will be successful.

Jennings and Haist find that performance measures have the greatest impact when

- they are thought to be accurate;
- the staff are dedicated to the purposes of the agency;

- top officials really care about and use performance measures;
- elected and politically appointed officials give performance measures attention and use them to shape agency management and policy; and
- increased human and financial resources are actually applied to performance goals.

Jennings and Haist found that performance measures are most effective under the following conditions:

- when the agency has control over outcomes;
- the performance measure is implemented close to the level of service delivery;
- the performance measures enhance an agencies mission;
- the performance measures are compatible with agency skills, tasks, and resources;
- leaders believe in them, because leadership matters; and
- the agency has high mission valence.

When these criteria are met, management is more focused on results, agency accountability is improved, and services are improved.

However, there are these critical cautions, concerns, and dangers:

- an agency might be held accountable for outcomes beyond its control;
- there may be little connection between performance and funding, beyond lip service;
- the gathering and maintaining of performance data can be overly costly and time consuming;
- there is much difficulty in measuring things that do not happen, such as how much crime was prevented or how many terrorists were stopped;
- there may be goal displacement; and most important,
- there can be failure to ask this question: performance for whom? An agency might perform especially well for some and very badly for others.

This little review of the findings of the systematic study of performance measurement and management reform can inform the challenges faced by OMB and by the agencies as they attempt to get to green. Performance measurement in government is the modern language by which we make and implement policy. We now know more about agency management and effectiveness than we have ever known before, and that information is far more transparent and available than ever before. Program management in the federal government is in serious trouble and in desperate need of both political and career leadership, of attention, and, above all, of resources. Whether the report carding approach can be reasonably expected to help agencies improve their management and get to green only time will tell.

Spreadsheets, Management, and the Challenges of Public Sector Performance

If I had a spreadsheet,
I'd spreadsheet in the mornin',
I'd spreadsheet in the evenin',
All over this land.
(All together now)
I'd spreadsheet out inefficiency,
I'd spreadsheet out waste,
I'd spreadsheet out correlation between my metrics and my budgets,
All over this land.

Lee Hays and Pete Seeger, in their wonderful folk song "If I Had a Hammer," sought to focus our minds and emotions on freedom and justice. With this rather crude adaptation of the first stanza of that classic, we seek to make a smaller but nevertheless important point. In many public administration circles the contemporary hammer of choice is the spreadsheet. Originally designed as analytic tools, spreadsheets have steadily become a surrogate for management. Spreadsheet software is included in virtually every desktop computer, thereby equipping every analyst and wannabe manager with a hammer and as the technological imperative tells us, when one has a hammer, everything looks like a nail.

133

Spreadsheets are a form of technology and there has always been a close connection between technology and management. Recall that the early Hawthorne studies were of the productivity of workers building small electric motors. Also recall that the primary finding was that manipulating how workers were managed was far more important to productivity than was manipulating the technological details of their work. Years later, W. Edwards Deming showed Japanese automakers and others how to apply Hawthorne-like principles to their management—he called it total quality management (TQM)—and thereby improved performance. In both the Hawthorne and TQM cases, to know what worked best managerially and in terms of performance, there had to be data and those data had to be timely, accurate, and relevant.

Spreadsheets and other applications of modern information technology are very powerful tools for gathering, managing, storing, and retrieving data. Spreadsheets are now the preferred instruments for both public and private sector data management. These tools have had a profound influence on contemporary thinking in the public sector. As Beryl Radin puts it in *Beyond Machiavelli: Policy Analysis Comes of Age*: If there is a single theme that characterizes the public sector in the 1990s, it is the demand for performance. A mantra has emerged in this decade, heard at all levels of government that calls for documentation of performance and explicit outcomes of government action. Spreadsheet based performance information is now a primary instrument for assessing government effectiveness as well as holding public officials accountable. Indeed there are now laws such as the Government Performance and Results Act of 1993 (GPRA) that require agency level performance measurement. The holy grail of performance measurement advocates and enthusiasts is to link annual measures of agency performance to their budget requests. Those associated with public sector performance measurement have taken to referring to what they do as "performance management." This suggests that performance is management or, at the very least, performance can be understood to be management and management can be understood to be performance. At the risk of being accused of dichotomous thinking, we suggest that there are very important differences between performance measurement and management.

The data gathering and management challenges associated with the development of reliable data, particularly data involving multiple agencies and jurisdictions, are daunting. Nevertheless, the promises of improved performance associated with better information are beguiling. Simple rationality suggests that the more we know and the more reliable our knowledge, the more likely we are to make wise decisions. The problem in the public sector is, of course, that program and management rationality are not the same thing as political rationality.

Spreadsheets and other forms of information management have been around long enough now to enable researchers to evaluate their reliability. After a lengthy and detailed study of spreadsheet reliability in business, Raymond R. Pantko concluded, in "What We Know About Spreadsheet Errors," in the *Journal of End User Computing*, that research done to date in spreadsheet development presents a very disturbing picture. "Every study that has attempted to measure errors, without exception, has found them at rates that would be unacceptable in any organization.... With such high cell error rates, most large spreadsheets will have multiple errors ... this will mean that many corporate decisions would be made on the basis of questionable analysis." Even with improvements in spreadsheet training and cell auditing, which can reduce errors, Pantko,'s research suggests considerable caution in relying on spreadsheet generated measures of public agency performance. It is useful to remember that Fannie Mae recently went through a major political and administrative shakeup partly blamed on an honest mistake made in a spreadsheet. This mistake, it is claimed, was a $1.2 billion accounting error.

On the upside, any serious reading of annual GPRA agency reports serves to indicate that we know far more than ever before about how federal agencies are performing, even if there are errors in the data. Whether improved knowledge in turn improves agency policy-making and management is an open question. The performance management approach in the federal government is made further complicated by the introduction by the Bush administration of linkages between annual performance data (Program Assessment Rating Tool—PART) and score-card systems (President's Management Agenda—PMA). Using spread-sheets developed in the PART process, the Office of Management and Budget is grading program performance (PMA) based on a combination of generally acceptable public management criteria as well as what many would regard the management and policy preferences of the Bush administration. Many old (Clinton administration) GPRA performance measures have been trumped by better PART scorecard measures as the Bush administration seeks leverage to induce agencies in the directions of their management and policy preferences.

Just as information technology has improved, so too has our knowl-edge of the organization and management of effective, high performing government agencies. In their brilliant synthesis of the research litera-ture on public sector management—"Galloping Elephants: Developing Elements of a Theory of Effective Government Organizations," in the *Journal of Public Administration Research and Theory*—Hal Rainey and Paula Steinbauer demonstrate that high performing public agencies have the following characteristics: oversight authorities that are support-ive, delegative, and attentive; supportive interest groups that are geo-graphically dispersed; favorable public support; carefully managed rela-tions between allies and partners; high mission valence; strong organi-zational cultures; leadership characterized by stability, effective goal set-ting, commitment to mission and skilled at administrative and political coping; and high levels of public service and mission motivation in their staff. The keys to public sector performance and effectiveness are very different depending on whether one is following the logic of perform-ance management or studying the results of research on effective gov-ernmental agencies. Performance measurement is one thing and effec-tive program management is another.

The wisdom of Carolyn Heinrich puts these differences in perspec-tive. Our "demand for performance" documentation should focus more on what public managers can learn about how to improve performance and less on the precise measurement of performance levels or "bottom-line" outcomes.

Book Six
Public Administration in the Era of Blurred Boundaries

Public Administration in the Era of Blurred Boundaries

The most important problem facing our field and profession is this: For whom do modern public administrators work?

There was a time when the answer to that question was obvious; we work for the jurisdictions that pay us. In our time, however, the answer to that question is not only no longer obvious, the answer is in very serious play. This is because there is an increasing disconnect between the problems and opportunities people have on one hand and the capacities of the governmental jurisdictions they live in to deal with problems and provide opportunities on the other hand. Our social, economic, and political problems will simply not stay within the boundaries of our jurisdictions.

The mismatch between jurisdictions and problems puts one in mind of this wise observation once made about universities: The world has problems, the university has departments. Put in the context of cities, states, and nations, I suggest that the world has problems, the people have jurisdictions.

Particularly obvious among the problems that defy national jurisdictional boundaries are stateless terrorism, unregulated global commerce, environmental degradation and pollution, contagious diseases (particularly AIDS), electronic communications (particularly the Internet), stateless criminal gangs and mobs, poverty and malnutrition, and drugs. Many of these same problems disobey the boundaries of the multiple jurisdictions—cities, counties, school districts, and special districts—that make up American metropolitan areas. Theorists describe our present circumstances as the fragmented state, the disarticulated state, the end of geography, the borderless state or even the end of the state. As the borders of cities and states and the sovereignty of nations decline in importance, there is a corresponding decline in the capacity of jurisdictions to contain some public policy issues and, therefore, in the jurisdiction's capacity to "manage" them. Because public administration is still mostly jurisdictionally based, many of the problems and issues we face appear beyond our reach.

To cope with the mismatch between jurisdictional boundaries and problems, public administrators at all levels of government practice administrative conjunction. Administrative conjunction is best understood as area-wide formal and informal horizontal and vertical linkages and patterns of cooperation between public service professionals representing area-wide jurisdictions. Public administrators practice conjunction with their professional counterparts out of a deep understanding that many public problems can only be dealt with effectively through jurisdictional cooperation, and out of a strong sense of jurisdictional interdependence. Studies of the practices of interjurisdictional networking indicate that leaders spend from 10 to 25 percent of their time outside their jurisdictions in patterns of conjunction with their counterparts.

Because they are paid by jurisdictions, how do top public administrators rationalize spending significant portions of their time on conjunction? First, they engage in interjurisdictional conjunction to address problems that cannot be jurisdictionally contained in an effort to reduce collective uncertainty and increase the prospects for problem solving. Second, they engage in conjunction based on legitimating professional assumptions of expertise, knowledge, and shared beliefs. Third, while top public administrators work for their jurisdictions and serve the people of those jurisdictions, it appears that they practice conjunction in order to serve a larger, inchoate public. Fourth, top public managers engaged in conjunction appear to practice a form of representation, along the lines of the logic of representative bureaucracy. But, the practice of conjunction is not just the representation of jurisdiction residents. It is the pursuit of a more generalized public interest extending well beyond jurisdictional borders. Fifth, public administrators practice conjunction in the shadows of their jurisdictional hierarchies, forgoing time given to internal management for time given to interjurisdictional networking. Sixth, the practice of conjunction allows public managers to preserve jurisdictional integrity while they work with other professionals to ameliorate problems that cannot be jurisdictionally contained.

The best examples of administrative conjunction can be found in American metropolitan areas. In most metropolitan areas the police chiefs, fire chiefs, public works directors, librarians, parks and recreation directors, social service directors, and the like, are both formally and informally networked in elaborate patterns of cooperation. In the absence of a single metropolitan jurisdiction and one hierarchy, it is patterns of administrative conjunction that increase the prospects for metropolitan-wide governmental effectiveness. Because there are no formal political leaders chosen by all of the people of the metropolitan area, there is not a legitimate metropolitan polity. The practices of democratic politics remain, with few exceptions, jurisdictionally based—city by city by city. There are formalized patterns of cooperation such as councils of government and some metropolitan areas have adopted area-wide special districts for air pollution control, and the like. And, there are a few actual consolidated metropolitan governments. But in the main, it is professional public administrators practicing conjunction that knit the metropolitan area together.

Administrative conjunction appears to be rather like light-weight bridges; they require solid grounding at each end, grounding in the jurisdictions. And, like light-weight bridges, each pattern of conjunction has a limited carrying capacity. But, in a metropolitan area, for example, there are dozens or even hundreds of these light-weight bridges, and combined they can make surprisingly flexible yet strong and enduring networks.

To return to the big question posed at the beginning, in the face of problems that cannot be jurisdictionally contained, for whom do public administrators work? We work for our jurisdictions and for a larger public and a greater public interest.

Public Administration and Jurisdiction

What is the biggest problem in American public administration? I surveyed the most recent books and articles in the field, had some conversations with trusted friends, both academic and practitioners, and with apologies to the artist formerly known as The Artist Formerly Known as Prince, settled on this rather discouraging title for the lecture: "A Brief Contemplation on the Subject Formerly Known as Public Administration." In my survey and conversations I found governance, networks, globalization, civil society, privatization, performance measurement, principals and agents, transparency, and a lot more. But, I had real trouble finding public administration. At the center of why it is so difficult to find public administration in modern America is the rapidly changing nature of our public jurisdictions.

Classic public administration was built on the assumption of jurisdiction, including the nation-state, states, cities, counties, regional agencies and special districts. From the logic of jurisdiction flows all of the essentials for the development of a professional merit-based civil service, a public administration. First, jurisdiction is specific to locale, a particular physical place circumscribed by arbitrary but invisible lines defining everything inside those lines as part of the jurisdiction. Second, within these lines the officials of jurisdictions govern, which is to say they exercise sovereign authority, make and enforce laws, tax and provide services to the people. Third, the logic of jurisdiction assumes a reciprocal relationship between the governed and those who govern. The preferred form of that reciprocal relationship we call democratic self-government, a jurisdictional arrangement by which the people select their leaders, who in return see after the interests of the people. Fourth, the logic of jurisdiction also assumes a reasonable match-up between people's needs and the capacity of the jurisdiction to meet those needs. The preferred form for organizing and managing the day-to-day reciprocal relationship between the governed and those who govern them we call professional public administration. Fifth, in classic public administration the jurisdiction is our employer and the house in which we work.

We believe we work in the people's house and that our role in this house is to serve them. Public administration is not just a job.

If there is a fundamental reason why it is so hard to find public administration these days it is the rapidly changing characteristics of jurisdictions, the people's houses.

The sovereignty of jurisdictions, and particularly nation-states, is evaporating out the top, leaking out the sides and seeping out the bottom. Threats to our national security are as likely to come from stateless terrorist groups as from other countries. Changes in the European and Asian economies are as likely to influence our economy as vice versa. The global economy challenges jurisdictionally based systems of taxation, particularly as more transactions are made over the Internet. And, because of the Internet, American laws against, for example, child pornography and gambling are extremely difficult to enforce. The mobility of capital is so great that nation-states, states, and cities now constitute markets in which firms shop for low wages, favorable tariffs, tax breaks, and lax regulation. With the freedom of human mobility, both physically and literally, people with resources can find places favorable to their interests, homes abroad, off-shore tax shelters, and the like.

When combined, these and other forces constitute a growing disconnection between jurisdictions and the capacity of jurisdictions to manage the problems their people face.

Jurisdictions have fixed boundaries; boundaries usually established many years ago for reasons that may no longer make sense. There is now a widely acknowledged mismatch between jurisdictional boundaries and jurisdictional problems. At the level of the nation-state, Daniel Bell describes it this way: "[T]he nation-state is becoming too small for the big problems of life, and too big for the small problems of life. It is too small for the big problems because there are no effective international mechanisms to deal with such things as capital flows, commodity imbalances, the loss of jobs, and the several demographic tidal waves that will be developing in the next 20 years. It is too big for the small problems because the flow of power to a national political center means that the center becomes increasingly unresponsive to the variety and diversity of local needs. In short, there is a mismatch in scale. In American metropolitan areas, high levels of suburbanization and jurisdictional fragmentation have deeply eroded the capacity of center cities to deal with their problems. Rural county lines drawn in the era of the horse and buggy now make little sense. The problems faced by the least advantaged of us—crime, drugs, little or no public transportation, chronic underemployment, inadequate affordable housing, air and water pollution—tend not to stay put and ignore arbitrarily drawn jurisdictional boundaries. The match between jurisdictions and the problems faced by those who live in jurisdictions is getting weaker and weaker. Short of war and scandal, it is politically very difficult to change jurisdictional boundaries.

Finally, jurisdictions themselves have increasingly degovermentalized by privatizing and contracting-out their services. At the federal level there are now eight contract employees for every civil servant.

Taken together, the changing forces affecting jurisdictions make it increasingly difficult to find public administration, let alone define and understand it.

Donald F. Kettl's very good book, *The Transformation of Governance: Public Administration for Twenty-first Century America* is a brave attempt to make sense of all of this. Based primarily on his study of the American national government, Kettl suggests that jurisdictionally based public administration rooted in hierarchies of authority and command and control structures is on the way out. In the context of rapidly changing jurisdictions, public administration is becoming governance, by which he means variously: the management of the links between government and its broader political, social and economic environment; government [substitute "jurisdiction"] may still act with authority and create formal obligations but increasingly public administration as governance is the management of the institutions and processes through which social action occurs, which may or may not be governmental; government [substitute "jurisdiction"] refers to the functions of public institutions while governance is the way government gets it done, often these days through nongovernmental means.

How shall governance be successfully done? Following Kettl, governance calls for a better fit between hierarchies of authority and governance; put another way, a better fit between public administration and the changing characteristics of jurisdictions. Following the logic of governance, public administration is changed to the management of linked jurisdictions and extended chains or networks of third-party service providers. Jurisdictional authority is to be replaced by the direction of interpersonal and intergovernmental processes. Information is replacing authority as the centerpiece of governance. According to Kettl, these are the building blocks of governance, the subject formerly known as public administration.

Public Administration, Governance, and the Concept of Universal Jurisdiction

Twentieth century American public administration was built on assumptions of territorial jurisdictional authority—the nation-state and the sub-jurisdictions of the nation-state—cities, counties, states. This public administration was also built on assumptions of territorially bounded formal state constitutions, democratic elections, and jurisdictional authority, usually exercised by public administrators. We act for the jurisdictions we work for, our actions legitimized by the state. In the twenty-first century one of the key assumptions upon which modern public administration was built no longer holds. Jurisdictions of all types—nation-states, states, counties—are losing their boundaries. In this global era many economic activities are no longer local and are increasingly forms of multijurisdictional or nonjurisdictional investments, production, and consumption sometimes called the end of economic geography. The revolution in telecommunication has forever altered the meaning of physical space and thereby forever altered the importance of borders and boundaries. The capacity of the state and its sub-jurisdictions to contain and thereby deal with complex social, economic and environmental issues has eroded significantly. As the borders and sovereignty of jurisdictions decline in importance, there is a corresponding decline in the capacity of jurisdictions to contain significant policy issues and therefore in the jurisdictions' ability to manage them. One defining principle of democratic theory is a congruence or symmetry between the governed and those who govern. It is very difficult to conceptualize representative democracy when many important decisions that affect the lives of the represented are often not controlled or even influenced by those who represent them. Taken together the declining salience of borders, the leakage of jurisdictional sovereignty and the disconnection between policy problems and jurisdictional capacity are referred to as the disarticulation of the state.

These points are widely known and understood. What is not understood is how the reality of the disarticulated state is affecting the practices and concepts of public administration. How is public administration to be defined when the city, the state and the nation-state are declining in relevance and when jurisdictional sovereignty is in doubt? It might be clear which jurisdictions pay which public administrators, but, given the disarticulation of the state, it is less and less clear for whom particular public administrators actually work.

Although hardly a definitive answer to the questions just posed, the contemporary use of the term governance in public administration comes closest to an answer. In very general terms governance in public administration is taken to mean extra-jurisdictional networks of rules, understandings, norms and procedures that seek to regularize behavior and control its effects. In most cases governance networks are managed by jurisdictionally based public administrators acting extra-jurisdictionally and collectively. While some public administrators work for formalized cooperative organizations based on agreements between jurisdictions, such as councils of governments in American metropolitan areas, the European Union and the United Nations, compared to jurisdictionally based public administrators they are rare. Governance networks vary widely in the degree of their density, longevity, and influence. All governance networks seek to reduce jurisdictional uncertainty by establishing procedures by which the expectations and preferences of actors representing many jurisdictions can converge. Jurisdictionally based public administrators, following governance network procedures, work together to deal with problems that cannot be jurisdictionally contained.

The problem is, of course, that in their practices of governance, public administrators usually lack a democratic warrant. Because democratic legitimacy is only jurisdictionally based, when public administrators act together in nonterritorial and extra-jurisdictional governance networks, they can only claim democratic legitimacy when they take their agreements and understanding to their separate jurisdictions for ratification by popularly elected state officials. It is widely acknowledged that most of the work of public administrators in governance networks is without the formal sanction of their elected principals, although it is doubtful that many administrators in their practice of governance stray far beyond the preferences of their principals. Because governance networks are not democratic electoral polities, how can the work of public administrators acting in such networks be democratically sanctioned?

One possible answer is the concept of universal jurisdiction taken from international jurisprudence. The logic of universal jurisdiction can be traced to the days of high-seas piracy as a justification for national navies to board pirate ships at sea, well beyond the boundaries of their countries. After the Second World War the Allied nations exercised the logic of universal jurisdiction to prosecute individuals for crimes against humanity committed beyond their borders as well as within their borders. In recent years universal jurisdiction has been exercised by Spain against Augusto Pinochet for crimes against Chileans in Chile while he was president. The United States prosecuted Manuel Noriega for crimes against both Americans and Panamanians while he was a Panamanian official and he is now in prison in the United States. The International Criminal Court of the United Nations administers treaty based agreements to prosecute state officials who are accused of torture, murder, and other forms of human rights violation.

The present use of the logic of universal jurisdiction is reactive and legal, an instrument used to punish those officials who have engaged in human rights violations against their own citizens. But, the logic of universal jurisdiction could be useful to modern public administration as a democratic rationale for the extra-jurisdictional practices of governance. Consider, for example, police chiefs and sheriffs in a metropolitan area operating in an extended governance network to collectively deal with gangs, drug traffic, hot pursuit, and other law enforcement challenges that cannot be jurisdictionally contained. In the absence of a metropolitan area democratic electoral polity, can there be, nevertheless, a universal jurisdiction of principles and understandings implemented by like-minded public administration professionals in the position of broadly "representing" a metropolitan area-wide universal jurisdiction? At the national level ministers (or secretaries) of environmental affairs work together to develop protocols to deal with air and water pollution, sometimes in the implementation of treaties, but often in the absence of formal treaties.

Classic public administration is based on the logic of delegated democratic authority practices within the fixed territory of a jurisdiction. Modern public administration may need to invent other kinds of jurisdictions—universal jurisdictions of principles. Such universal jurisdictions are actually all around us in the form of public administrators "representing" classic territorially based jurisdictions actively engaged in cooperative interjurisdictional networks of governance. Together, in the shadows of their territorially based authority, they formulate the principles of universal jurisdictions and cooperate to implement them. While there may not be classic democratic electoral polities that comprehend whole metropolitan areas, whole regions of the world, or the whole world, there are elaborate forms of governance and universal jurisdiction.

Quasi-Governmental Organizations

What, you ask, is a *quango*? In the British branch of the English language, a quango is an adaptation of the American phrase: "quasi-non-governmental organization." The phrase was originally used in the 1970s by Alan Pifer, then president of the Carnegie Corporation, who wished to refer to a new kind of organization established by the federal government and performing some role or task for the federal government while being separately constituted as a "private organization." He had in mind particularly the Tennessee Valley Authority, the Bonneville Power Authority, and the Port Authority of New York and New Jersey. To abbreviate the phrase "quasi-non-governmental organization," Anthony Barker, the esteemed British scholar, first used the acronym "quango" and although the word has not been used widely in the United States it has stuck like superglue in the United Kingdom.

Almost every issue of the leading newspapers in the U.K. has an article or editorial about quangos—most of them critical. The word "quango" is, according to W. J. M. Mackenzie, a "barbarism" subject to modifications that would make even an amateur philologist blush—as in "a new ruling class of quangocrats," or the people are treated as if they are at a "quangroo court." The House of Lords has been referred to as a quango—a "Quaintly Archaic Near-Gerontocratic Organization." There have been attacks from outer space by the quango people and the Conservative Party has committed quangocide. And, finally, one particularly acerbic observer claims that quango means a "quite unacceptable and nasty government offshoot."

What, exactly, is a quango? The *Oxford English Dictionary* defines a quango as "an organization with financial support from and senior appointments made by the government, but not controlled by it." To confuse things further, in the U.K., quangos are also sometimes known as "non-departmental public bodies," or NDPBs—an unpronounceable acronym. Because it sounds slightly derisive and moves rhythmically across the tongue, the word "quango" has stuck. The quangos themselves have also stuck, proving to be at least as difficult to kill as formal agencies.

In the United Kingdom, there are now more than one thousand quangos, ranging from trivial advisory groups such as the Apple and Pear Council and the Place Names Committee to large and powerful executive bodies such as the Public Health Laboratory Service and the area health delivery trusts of the National Health Service. Most

British quangos operate at the regional and local level. As creations of government, quangos are not a blend of the public and private sectors or the application of market-based logic to government services. They are, instead, simply a nondepartmental way to organize government services.

In the United States, the modern preferred term is "hybrid" organizations—organizations created by government but resembling privately owned, profit-seeking businesses. They charge fees for their services and attempt to cover their expenses. Like quangos, the boards of directors of hybrids are appointed rather than elected. Like quangos, hybrids are exempted from many standard departmental rules and regulations and their employees are not part of the civil service. And, like quangos, hybrids are single purpose bodies rather than comprehensive general bodies of government. But, they are government, nevertheless, and big government at that. According to Jonathan GS Koppel in his excellent new book *The Politics of Quasi-Government: Hybrid Organizations and the Dynamics of Bureaucratic Control*, the combined liability of federal hybrids is over $2 trillion, more than the entire budget for one year. There are more than 50 major federal hybrids, the best known being the TVA, the Federal Home Loan Mortgage Corporation (Freddie Mac), the Federal National Mortgage Association (Fannie Mae). There are hundreds of state and local hybrids, often known as special districts, the best known being the larger metropolitan airport authorities. Some American hybrids, such as Freddie Mac and Fannie Mae, are actually profit-making stockholder corporations backed by the federal government.

Globalization has produced an important emerging form of quangos or hybrids—international organizations such as the World Bank (WB) and the International Monetary Fund (IMF)—funded by governments but making loans like private banks. The conditions set out for loans, particularly to underdeveloped countries, essentially require those countries to operate their economies according to WB or IMF criteria. There are interesting smaller examples of hybrids, such as the World Intellectual Property Organization and the Internet Corporation for Assigned Names and Numbers.

The initial reasons for setting up quangos in the U.K. and hybrids in the United States are very nearly the same: to concentrate on one purpose; to develop the expertise to meet that purpose; to be at arms length from departments and their hierarchies; to be more flexible and responsive; to be independent from the cut and thrust of politics; to regionally or nationally transcend traditional jurisdictional boundaries; to overcome gridlock and slowness associated with the separation of powers; to involve stake holders, clients, and interest groups; and to be businesslike. And the critique of quangos in the U.K. and hybrids in the United States is also very nearly the same: Their leaders are unelected and unaccountable; they are secretive; they are unresponsive, particularly to local preferences; they fragment government and make it difficult for citizens to understand government; the appointments of their directors are secretive, unfair, and constitute a modern form of patronage; they can sometimes ignore standard governmental constraints regarding due process, fairness, and equity; they were often put in place at a particular time to structurally lock in the preferences of those in political power at that time; once established they become interest groups and lobbyists and their numbers and power keep growing.

Why are quangos in the U.K. so controversial while American hybrids, except in crises such as the savings and loan scandals of the 1980s, are of little interest to the public? The answer appears to be that British quangos tend to operate at the regional and local levels and are often engaged in service delivery not unlike cities. Cities, of course, are democratically controlled by their residents while quangos are not. Quangos are more easily controlled centrally, which explains why members of Parliament, despite their claims to the contrary, tend to favor them. To improve the rather bad image of quangos at the local level a series of reforms have been proposed, such as requiring open meetings and publishing the minutes of those meetings; requiring annual reports and balance sheets; causing departmental ministers to re-examine the quangos related to their departments toward the possibility of elimination or consolidation; and requiring quangos to practice fairness, justice, and equity in their personnel practices. Doubtless the most thorough and interesting books on British quangos is Chris Skelcher's *The Appointed State*.

Although there is a very good literature on American quasi-governments—particularly the Koppell book referred to above, the recent Tom Stanton book, *Government-Sponsored Enterprises*, and a series of articles and books by Harold Seidman and Ronald Moe—the subject is thought to be arcane and dull. This is a great pity because hybrid quasi-governments are increasingly important parts of American governance.

Both British and American students of quasi-governments generally agree that when they are compared to traditional departmental forms of organization, hybrids are more difficult to control politically. There are, however, forms of accountability other than accountability to elected bodies—accountability to clients, to the law, to the public interest—and quasi-governments vary widely along these dimensions. There is little doubt that, like ordinary bureaucratic organizations, hybrid organizations can engage in goal displacement and can take care of their own interests at the expense of the public interest, the recent dust-up over executive salaries and benefits as Freddie Mac being a case in point. But hybrid organizations will remain attractive to policy makers at all levels of government, including the international level. As Koppell claims, they will almost certainly play a prominent role in future governance, particularly international governance. The accountability problems of quangos and hybrids will be even more vexing. So, we will all need to learn to quango, and it would be best if we learn to quango properly.

Whither Europe: Will the European Union Survive?

It may come as a surprise to learn that *The Federalist Papers* and *The Writings of the Anti-Federalists* are at the top of the reading lists of European public officials and government scholars. Europeans are not reading the debates of the founding fathers in a burst of pro-Americanism—indeed this is a period of particularly loud and sharp criticism of the United States virtually throughout Europe. American federalism literature is being read because it is particularly relevant to the biggest political-governmental issue in Europe—the future of the European Union (EU).

Over the past half-century the countries of Western Europe have moved steadily in the direction of federation. First, the 15 countries in the EU voted to admit over the next three years 10 more countries. Second, under the presidency of Valery Giscard d' Estaing, the Convention on the Future of Europe completed its work, adopting a draft treaty establishing a Constitution for Europe. The Preamble of the draft Constitution reads in part: "Convinced that, while remaining proud of their own national identities and history, the peoples of Europe are determined to transcend their ancient divisions and, united ever more closely, to forge a common destiny."

According to the draft Constitution, all five of the presently established institutions of the European Union are to be continued—the European Parliament, the European Council (the heads of state of the 15 member states), the Council of Ministers (the ministers of each cabinet-level department from each state), the European Commission (a president and a minister of foreign affairs chosen by the European Council and 13 members selected by rotation from the member states), and the Court of Justice.

Of these institutions, it is the European Commission that serves as the executive arm of the European Union, administering programs, exercising coordination, executing budgets, and proposing legislation to the European Parliament, to which it is primarily responsible.

As is always the case in federalism, the divisive issues in the EU have to do with what ought to be the powers of each of these five institutions vis-à-vis the powers of the member states. In the United States we refer to states rights and unfunded mandates to describe what ought to be locally retained powers and federal encroachment on them. In the language of the EU, allocations of power to the Union and to the member states are justified on the basis of so-called competencies, those matters that are understood to be the exclusive competence of the EU such as monetary policy and diplomatic policy, those matters that are understood to be the exclusive competence of member states such as law enforcement and education, and those matters involving shared competence such as internal markets, transportation, energy, environmental affairs, and the like. It is in the details of sorting out competencies that the divisive issues of federalism play themselves out. And, it is in these details that we find public administration.

A very good example of these issues is found in the Alternative Report signed by a group of members of the European Convention who disagree with the draft Constitution. They argue that "the transfer of more decision making power from member states to the Union, concerning criminal justice matters and new areas of domestic policy, will make the Union more remote. The new category of 'shared competencies' gives no assurance how power is to be shared, particularly as member states will be forbidden to legislate in those areas if the Union decides to act. The Union is behaving too bureaucratically. The European institutions should be less unwieldy and rigid. The constitution concentrates more executive and budgetary power in the very EU institutions which have been the subject of repeated and continuing scandals over mismanagement, waste and fraud."

Rather than a constitution expanding the powers of the EU vis-à-vis the member states, this minority report proposes that the EU be discontinued, replaced by the Europe of Democracies (ED), a cooperative association or partnership in which member states must each approve laws under consideration by the ED and by which the legislatures of member states choose the commissioners of the ED. This expression of sentiments—a mixture of distaste for the bureaucratic way EU policy is made and administered, and opposition to making any of the powers of their own countries subsidiary to the powers of the EU—generally captures the position of those opposed to the proposed new constitution for the EU.

In virtually every conversation about the EU, the phrase "the Brussels bureaucracy" is used, and there are regular references to EU corruption, references based on a few rather high profile cases of fraud and graft by EU operatives. Although there is no doubt that the administration of the EU can be bureaucratic, what "the Brussels bureaucracy" really means is opposition at the level of the member state to the exercise of central EU authority. It is both easier and more evocative to complain about how an EU policy is being implemented than it is to logically argue against that policy.

The logic of federalism is to secure a relationship between jurisdictions desiring union without seeking unity. In such a relationship legal sovereignty is in some form divided between two layers of government. As we know from the American experience, this division of sovereignty is highly dynamic and continually controversial. It is argued, for example, that the full realization of American federalism did not happen until the Civil War and the passage of the 13th, 14th, and 15th amendments, 75 years after the ratification of the Constitution. In the 140 years since, the relative powers of the national government and the state governments have waxed and waned depending on the times and the issues. Today our elected officials are fond of the phrase "the American people," a particularly serviceable expression that reflects our general sentiments. The proposed constitution for the EU uses the phrase "the European peoples," an honest reflection of the rather limited commitment of many Europeans to the EU and a fair expression of popular sentiment in Europe.

The United States, France, the United Kingdom, and Denmark are examples of sovereign states, but Idaho and Delaware are not. What, then, is the European Union? Does it have "stateness"? Ronald L. Watts, in *Comparing Federal Systems*, describes the EU as a confederation rather like the United States under the Articles of Confederation. Nevertheless, according to Watts, the EU has taken on most of the qualities of a sovereign state. David McKay, in *Designing Europe: Comparative Lessons from the Federal Experience*, agrees, describing the EU as "an evolving species of federal state, albeit a highly decentralized one. European Union citizenship now exists even if the loyalty of most Europeans remains with national and regional governments rather than with the federal government." Vernon Bogdanor disagrees for two reasons. First, "even if we were to call the EU a federation, it would be a federation of a very peculiar kind. It would be a commercial federation, but not a federation from the point of view of foreign policy and defense.... A further element vital, surely, to a federal government is that the central authority should have command over sufficient financial resources to allow it to exercise effective authority over the component units.... It would be wrong to define the EU as a form of federal government for a reason that is even more fundamental. It is, quite simply, that it is not a state, even though it possesses some of the appurtenances of a state. It lacks features, which all states possess. It has, for example, neither a head of state nor a head of government."

The positions of those for and those against the ratification of the proposed EU Constitution are echoes of the federalist-anti-federalist debates found in the literature left by the American founding fathers. Even if the proposed EU Constitution is ratified, however, most students of federalism and sovereignty believe that the jurisdictional powers of the member states will be relatively stronger than the powers of the Union. The inability of the EU to respond effectively to the crises in the Balkans in the 1990s is illustrative of the decentralized character of the Union and its weakness at the center. Nevertheless, development of the EU has been a remarkable achievement, having peacefully brought the countries of Europe closer together than they have ever been. Furthermore, the EU is a union of democracies. Today Europeans face the momentous question of whether to further formalize and strengthen their confederation by adopting the proposed Constitution and whether ratification will inexorably lead to a fully realized federal government like the United States.

Killing Missionaries: Some Lessons

In April 2001, with training and equipment provided by the United States government and with our support, a Colombian military jet shot down a small private airplane flying over the upper Amazon region in Colombia. The plane was carrying American missionaries, but the pilot of the Colombian military jet believed it was carrying drugs, so he shot it down, killing a woman and her child. Now both the State and Defense Departments claim that the Colombian jet pilot was told that this particular plane was not carrying drugs, and, of course, the Colombians deny these claims. Investigations are afoot. The Chattering Classes are flocking to TV talk shows, spinning the issue one way and then another.

Although unfortunate in the extreme for the missionary family, this case puts in bold relief some critical public policy issues.

First, there is a declining relationship between jurisdictional borders and the public problems faced by jurisdictions. Even with the fences, airplanes, jet boats, border patrols and satellite surveillance of the war on drugs, the United States evidently cannot get the enemy to surrender. There is no surrender in Los Angeles and no surrender in Colombia. Drugs, like air and water pollution, tend to ignore political lines. The same is true of organized crime. Economic activity, which was once at least somewhat local in the sense of being jurisdictionally contained, is increasingly multijurisdictional or nonjurisdictional. Investment, production and consumption are seldom geographically contained, and this trend is destined to continue. Furthermore, the most powerful modern instrument for communication and commerce, the Internet, does not obey political lines. A city, a state, or a nation-state may make laws assuming to regulate or control the Internet, but so far with little effect. Taxing Internet commerce is turning out to be very difficult. In the modern world there are global opportunities that transcend the nation-state, and there are global problems that ignore the nation-state and disobey its laws. How shall cities, states and nations make public policy and carry out that policy when the problems they face will not stay put? Is attempting to control drug traffic in the air over Colombia, as a matter of policy, the problem? Or, are we just not doing it right and that is the problem? Are dead American missionaries just collateral damage?

Second, sovereignty and citizenship, bedrock concepts of the nation-state, are in play. Susan Strange calls the decline of state sovereignty "the retreat of the state" and the "end of geography." Multinational corporations find the most favorable business environment (low wages, good workers, low taxes), move there, and stand ready to move again if things change. Is it, then, the country that is sovereign, or the corporation? Individuals and families are increasingly linked globally, making the passport less and less significant. Immigrants, legal and illegal, move across porous borders. Regional agreements such as the European Union and the North America Free Trade Agreement change the role of the traditional state, making trade and mobility easier. American missionaries, for example, get to Colombia fairly easily. English is becoming the international language of commerce and, to some, is threatening the indigenous languages and cultures of traditional nation-states. We appear to be inventing versions of national citizenship that recognize both declining national sovereignty and some nascent forms of regional (Europe, North American) and global citizenship.

Third, the fashion of the day is to contract public functions to nonprofit organizations and profit-making corporations. This is the so-called disarticulated or attenuated state. Governmental functions and services are now less often carried out by civil servants with clear responsibility to the sovereign, and more often, carried out by organizations or companies with, putting it gently, mixed allegiances. There were, for example, contractual relations, both formal and informal, between the United States and Colombia, to wage war on drugs. For whom, then, was that Colombian jet pilot working? It will be said that he was working for Colombia. Certainly he was. But was he not one of our mercenaries? In the era of the disarticulated state, issues of accountability are fuzzy, at best.

Fourth, politics, which is to say campaigns, parties, elections, office-holding, and law making, remain solidly jurisdictional. Because we have yet to invent effective and enduring systems of multijurisdictional or transjurisdictional politics, we are left with jurisdictional politics in a world that is increasingly nonjurisdictional. I once asked the former mayor of Kansas City, Missouri, Emanuel Cleaver, why the mayors of the many cities of the Kansas City metropolitan area did not appear to work together on area-wide problems. He answered, "I have no votes in the suburbs." Together we concluded that "all politics is local," as Speaker Tip O'Neill famously said, but that many problems are area-wide. There are, of course, metropolitan area councils of governments, just as there are regional agreements between nation-states. And there is the United Nations. But politics remains almost entirely jurisdictional. The war on drugs and agreements between the United States and Colombia have considerable local political traction. It is unwise for a politician to be soft on drugs. These are jurisdictional politics in the context of a problem that defies jurisdiction.

Fifth, the good news is that public administration is increasingly trans- and multi-jurisdictional. We recognize that many problems cannot be jurisdictionally contained and that the only way we can effectively deal with them is to work systematically with our counterparts in other jurisdictions. Unlike politicians, public administrators live in a world of "felt interdependence." In most metropolitan areas police chiefs have an organization and work closely together, as do fire chiefs, public works directors, city managers, librarians and so forth. So, while there are very few actual metropolitan governments in the United States, there are dozens of good examples of "metropolitan governance." While the public administrators who operate this governance actually work for and are paid by particular jurisdictions, they also think of themselves as working for everyone in the metropolitan area. They have figured out how to deal with the sovereignty issue. The same thing is happening with public administrators at the state and national levels. So, while politics remains stubbornly local, public administration is regionalizing and globalizing. Most of this regional and global activity is positive, dealing with issues that transcend borders. But not all regional and global public administration is good. The killing of the missionaries was a result of local American politics and policy and the implementation of that policy, in a disarticulated form, in the United States and Colombia. In this case the tension is between local politics and regional problems, and public administrators are caught in that tension. Nobody ever said public administration was easy.

Book Seven
All Public Administration is Local

Among the City Managers

Serious students of public administration know that council-manager form governments and city managers are among our favorite subjects. We like them because they represent much of what is ordinarily associated with the progressive and reform origins of public administration—professional management, merit civil service, public service distribution without favoritism, uncorrupt relations with vendors and contractors, efficiency, economy, and above all, a firewall between city politics and city administration. Council-manager form government in its pure and original form is the policy-administration dichotomy come alive.

For over thirty years I have been going to ICMA conferences. After three full days of attending and participating in panels, enjoying receptions, listening to speeches, and engaging in many hallway seminars at this conference, I can report the following:

First, we need not worry about the education, experience, qualifications, and dedication of American city managers. Taken together this is as impressive a group of professionals as I have ever been around. They know what they are doing and they do it very well. The demographic mix is increasingly impressive. There are as many young city managers and assistant city managers as there are senior long-time mangers. There are now many more women and minorities among city managers.

Second, the nature of the work of city managers continues to change and these changes are palpable. Ten years ago city managers were talking about and working on economic development. Now most of the panels and conversations have to do with responsiveness— responsiveness to neighborhoods, various kinds of communities, and political, economic, and social leaders. The concern for and interest in efficiency as the rationale for professional city administration has given way to a concern for neighborhoods, competing interests, problem solving, and above all, leadership.

Third, ICMA has changed over the years. In the 1960s the name was changed from the International City Managers' Association to the International City Management Association, recognition that ICMA was more than just the representation of the interests of city managers. This change was also recognition that professional city administration was taking many forms, including the administration of cities that do not have council-manager charters. An increasing number of the members of ICMA were not, in a strictly formal sense, city managers. They were chief administrative officers, or chief executives, or deputy mayors. Then, in the late 80s, ICMA changed its name again, this time to the International City/County Management Association, recognizing that local government is not just cities and that many members of ICMA had become professional county administrators.

Now ICMA appears to be in another period of fundamental transition. Many cities have modified the classic council-manager model by establishing a directly elected mayor, by changing from at-large to district council elections, by full-time paid mayors with staff, and in larger council-manager cities full-time paid council with staff. There are fewer and fewer classic-traditional council-manager form cities. In addition, many mayor form cities have adopted features of council-manager form government such as a professional executive, an established merit based civil service, and tight systems for the control over city contracts and vendors. As the research literature on the subject indicates, council-manager form cities and mayor form cities are gradually tending to resemble each other.

The dilemma for ICMA is this: How much of its energy should be spent on developing professional city administration for all forms of cities and counties, as against energy spent supporting and defending council-manager form government? Throughout its history ICMA has been not only a powerful force for the highest quality professional city administration, it has also been a strong voice for the council-manager form.

This issue was recently brought to a head by events in Cincinnati. A group of civic leaders proposed a charter change which would considerably strengthen the powers of the separately elected mayor while at the same time retaining a city manager but with much reduced powers. ICMA was called in to assess the proposed charter change and render an opinion as to whether these changes met ICMA criteria for recognition as a council-manager form city. The Cincinnati city manager was of the opinion that the proposed changes so watered down the council-manager form government that, if adopted, Cincinnati would be a council-manager form city in name only. ICMA decided not to oppose the charter change and it was passed by the voters. Because Cincinnati is a high profile council-manager form city, the charter change was a major subject of discussion among ICMA members. The question for ICMA members is: In the same way that ICMA works against charter referenda designed to drop council-manager form government in favor of mayor form government, should ICMA work against the adoption of proposed charter changes which modify council-manager government in fundamental ways? One small group of managers has formed the Stauton Society (named in honor of Stauton, Virginia, the first council-manager form city) for the purpose of defending council-manager government in more-or-less its pure form. The majority of ICMA members appear to prefer to work within the confines of the organization to sort through this question and try to find a new consensus.

Fourth, ICMA has long operated a system of recognition by which it recognizes local governments as having professional management. From 1914 until 1969 only cities with the classic council-manager form could be recognized. Many council-manager form cities were making important structural changes and many cities were appointing officials responsible for overall administrative affairs without adopting the council-manager form. In response ICMA added a second form of recognition—cities with general management positions such as chief administrative officer. The distinctions between the two can be fuzzy, and city structural changes appear to happen faster than ICMA can respond. Last revised fifteen years ago, the ICMA system of recognition is widely acknowledged to be in need of major revisions; indeed, one seasoned former city manager referred to criteria for recognition as a "train wreck." For example, the proper appointing power of city managers is described as "the full authority for the appointment and removal of at least most of the heads of the principal departments and functions," whereas the appointing power of general managers is to "exercise significant influence in the appointing of key administrative personnel." Figure *that* out.

There are fewer and fewer classic-manager form cities, therefore, more and more of the members of ICMA manage cities with non-classic features (directly elected mayors with power, council elected by district, full-time paid mayors and council, a fuzzy line between politics and administration, etc.) The structural details that combine to constitute a proper council-manager form city are neither clear nor agreed-upon, therefore ICMA recognition is losing its meaning. While ICMA continues its advocacy of council-manager forms of government as the ideal type, its emphasis is subtly shifting toward voluntary member credentialing, an emphasis that neatly sidesteps the form of government question. In fairness, many in ICMA leadership loudly disagree with these observations.

Fifth, ICMA voluntary credentialing is a state-of-the-art system of continuing education and manager self-assessment based on the logic of continual improvement. According to ICMA, "credentialing is different from certification. Credentialing means that a manager is measured against his or her peers and meets a standard, but also commits to continuous professional development. Certification, on the other hand, means that a minimum standard has been achieved and a certifying body declares that the certificant is minimally qualified." To date, fully 10 percent of ICMA's 8,000 members are credentialed, and there are many candidates in the queue. Younger managers appear to find the ICMA credentialing program especially appealing, in part because being credentialed is a form of qualification to manage or administer council-manager cities, mayor-council cities, and the increasing percentage of cities that mix the characteristics of the two. Voluntary credentialing is destined to be both a big ICMA success story and a splendid example of an effective professional association response to changing circumstances.

Sixth, although ICMA added the word "county" to its name in 1991 to reflect the county administrators among its members and to recognize increasing county government professionalism, the importance of county administrators in the organization is more recent. Indeed, three of the last four ICMA presidents have been county administrators.

Seventh, council-manager form government, albeit somewhat modified, is growing. From 1984 to 2000 the number of mayor form cities dropped from 3,786 to 2,988 while council manager government grew from 2,290 to 3,302 cities. But, several very high profile cities—Tampa, Oakland, San Diego, Spokane—dropped council-manager form government in favor of the strong mayor form. This has led several journalists to conclude that council-manager form government is in decline, when the opposite is true. Nevertheless it is not good news to advocates of council-manager government that several large cities have dropped "the plan," as it is called.

Eighth, unlike states and the national government, American cities modify and adapt their structures at a surprisingly rapid rate. It is the one level of government that the people like to tinker with. The changing structural terrain of American cities is a considerable challenge to city managers, a challenge they appear to handle very well.

There is little doubt that all of these changes leave the job of the typical city manager more difficult than it was twenty or even ten years ago. In many cities the firewall between politics and administration is a bit rusty and has a few holes—making administration a bit hotter. But this remarkable band of professionals seems more than up to it.

Ninth, ICMA has always enjoyed outstanding leadership. Mark E. Keane served brilliantly from 1967 until 1983 and is still active in association affairs. The remarkable Bill Hansel served from 1983 until 2002, guided the development of the voluntary credentialing program, and carefully navigated the winds and currents of the so-called "reform of the reform," ICMA-speak for managing in the context of modified or adapted versions of council-manager form government. The greatly respected Robert O'Neill Jr. recently took over and, with approval of the Executive Board, has initiated a strategic planning exercise to demonstrate the performance dividend of professional local government management and to answer this question: What value does the city management profession bring to communities and to local government organizations?

Tenth, American local government is widely admired in other countries, and several are copying elements of our approach, particularly the emphasis on professional management. The word "international" in ICMA was once thought to be a bit grand, but not today. For example there were many regular members from other countries at the San Diego conference, and several countries sent delegations to learn what they could.

Local government administrators are among the most professional, capable, and dedicated public administrators in the land, and in representing their interests; ICMA is a notably dynamic and effective association.

The Denial of Local Knowledge and the Assault on Professional Competence

In the modern world of shared power and diffuse accountability, public administration finds itself carried into a vortex of two particularly pernicious trends. First is the growing tendency on the part of officials in central governments that are part of federated and intergovernmental systems to deny the importance of local knowledge. Second is the continuing political assault on all forms of professional competence, particularly management competence. Each trend, by itself, is injurious to governmental effectiveness, but together they spell disaster, particularly in an era of shared power. Two examples, one domestic and one international, spring to mind.

We are nearing the end of a generation of reform of public education, not a grassroots reform growing up from the schools and the school districts, but a reform initially driven by the states and now, with the passage of No Child Left Behind, a major federal initiative. State legislators and governors as well as presidents and members of Congress have discovered that it is good politics to declare that many public schools are not effective, and it is particularly good politics to pass laws designed to fix schools. Although the advocates of reform, mostly politicians and consultants, squeal at the fact, modern education reform is freighted with the assumption that many if not most local school boards don't know what they are doing. Educational knowledge in Austin and Sacramento, and particularly Washington, D.C., trumps the collective knowledge of members of the local school boards in Dallas and Fresno. The whole purpose of local school boards is based on the primacy of local knowledge and local democratic control. However well meaning, contemporary education reform is a massive insult to that primacy and to any reasoned sense of effective policy making in federated systems.

It is not just local school boards that are judged by state and federal level reformers to be ineffective, so too are teachers, principals and superintendents. However well meaning, education reform is a massive insult to the logic of professional competence. In a wonderful recent survey by Emporia State University it was determined that people give the schools their children attend either an A or a B, but they give state legislators a D or an F. Now there is local knowledge for you.

The substance of the top-down education reform project is debatable and this is not the place for that debate. What is not debatable is that No Child Left Behind is a whopping unfunded mandate as are many of the state initiated education reforms. The states have a very legitimate claim regarding their role in local education reform because of their constitutional responsibilities for public education and because they are paying an ever increasing share of the costs. But the federal government has no such claim. Some states such as Vermont are openly rebelling against the federal government on this matter and others are quietly engaging in what could charitably be described as passive implementation of No Child Left Behind. Teachers and principals, bless them, are soldiering on; after all, they are the ones who are really trying not to leave any child behind. Rather than the top-down logic of No Child Left Behind, genuine education reform could have been hammered-out in serious processes of negotiation and collaboration between states and school boards and between states, school boards, and the federal government.

On the international front there are likewise examples of the denial of local knowledge and the assault on professional competence. In the 1990s one of the biggest challenges was to bring peace to Bosnia. This was accomplished by engaging both American and non-American professionals who knew the Balkans and could speak the languages. It was assumed that international organizations could be trusted and were legitimate partners in the Bosnian peace keeping effort. The peacekeeping effort followed the Dayton Peace Accords, agreements based on a process of mediation and compromise that engaged all relevant stakeholders. Once fighting had ceased, the peacekeeping effort was directed by the State Department. On the ground every effort was made to respect the integrity of Bosnian factions and their political and religious leaders and to try not to be seen as siding with one or the other. Rebuilding contracts were designed to directly involve locals in both their policy and execution. Local institutions and customs were understood to be legitimate and were supported. It was understood that change takes time and that Western notions of electoral democracy might not be fully applicable in the Bosnian situation. In short, local knowledge was taken very seriously as was professional competence. Negotiation, mediation, and collaboration were practiced in recognition of the realities of power sharing. Not one American has died in hostile action in Bosnia since the Dayton Peace Accords went into effect.

While acknowledging that Iraq is not Bosnia, comparisons are nevertheless informative. In a heated post-September 11, 2001, atmosphere, those convinced of the wisdom of pre-emptive war appear now to have been overly reliant on a few Iraqi ex-patriots for their intelligence and not sufficiently open to other sources of intelligence. The United Nations and particularly Hans Blix, the director of UN arms inspections, were openly ridiculed by American officials, as were officials in our key regional alliances such as NATO. There was no summit with our primary allies designed to hammer out a course of action on Iraq and the "coalition of the willing" ended up involving primarily minor U.S. allies. On virtually every key policy question the Defense Department trumped the State Department, and even after handing over sovereignty to the interim Iraqi government, DoD continues to run the show. Although the army had long been the primary stabilizing force in Iraq, in the early stages of the occupation it was disbanded and scattered. Military and contract specialists brought to Iraq to assist in rebuilding were and are experts in their fields but few of them know anything about Iraq, its culture, or its languages. At every stage in the run-up to the war, during the war, and now in the occupation, the United States has denied the salience of local knowledge. And at every stage the United States has been overly reliant on the judgments of a few top civilian officials in DoD, has not listened to military professionals, and has made spectators of our professional diplomats. And we are paying a very dear price.

In a world of shared power the lessons in both education reform and international affairs are these: Local knowledge matters, and policy and policy implementation is always best when it is based on negotiation, compromise, and mediation between central and local authorities. Professional competence matters, and policy works best when it is framed by elected officials who have listened carefully to experts, because, in the end, it is the experts at the local level who will be carrying out that policy.

How Did Local Public Administrators Become "First Responders"?

There was a time not that long ago when localities were mostly insulated from world affairs. No longer. There is little, maybe nothing that is national, international, or global that does not now have some sort of local manifestation. In terms of its ultimate effects, to borrow from

Tip O'Neill, all public administration is local.

James Rosenau, in his brilliant *Distant Proximities*, describes a world in which all significant distant events and issues have a local or proximate manifestation, and significant local events and issues influence other proximities. In two recent and popular treatments of distant proximities, Benjamin R. Barber's *Jihad vs. McWorld* and Thomas Friedman's *The Lexus and the Olive Tree*, the point is the interactions between local and regional cultures, particularly Islamic cultures and worldwide forces, particularly American popular culture and western capitalism. Contemporary terrorism is, for example, not primarily state sponsored but regionally organized and, when carried out, always local.

It is the local authorities, and particularly the professionals, now referred to as the first responders, who deal with terrorism as well as all other local manifestations of regional and global forces. It is, therefore, critically important that there be informed and effective local professionals and especially professionals who understand distant proximities and know how to engage in effective governance. According to Rosenau "distant circumstances will become ever more proximate.... [F]ragmentation will be with us for a long time, and surely many of its tensions will intensify. But inclinations to incorporate new, horizontal forms of authority into the panoply of governance mechanism are not lacking, and that is not a trivial conclusion." These horizontal and vertical intergovernmental mechanisms, all models of power sharing, are built and operated primarily by professional public executives, many of them at the local level.

It is fair to ask what ought to be the proper role of local appointed executives—city and county managers and administrators, school superintendents, authority executives—in this new governance. Local jurisdictions are, after all, little democracies and local appointed executives, however expert, do not in a formal sense represent the people. The problem is this: Politics is in almost all cases contained within the boundaries of jurisdictions and local elected officials tend to have a rather limited interest in matters of jurisdictional fragmentation and the institutional complexities in which cities are nested. Local elected officials live in jurisdictionally contained worlds of campaigns, elections, ordinance making, budget approving, and casework for citizens. Local politics is often innocent of the significance of distant proximities. Because of this, the practices of interjurisdictional governance and the arrangements for power sharing that are essential to local responsiveness to distant proximities are mostly left to professional administrators, a matter that brings us to this paradox: Many of the critical elements of local democratic governance depend for their effectiveness on nonelected professional administrators.

In large scale and formalized systems of power sharing, such as the European Union, this paradox is referred to as the "democratic deficit," and the functioning of the EU is frequently referred to as the "Brussels bureaucracy." The point is the same, however. Despite the growing importance of the EU, politics in Europe is still almost entirely contained within each member country, the politics of the EU itself being rather weak. The administration of the EU is, by comparison, rather strong, a strength largely based on the practices of administrative governance as power sharing. Some regional authorities in the United States resemble the EU in terms of formalization if not in terms of scale. But unlike the EU, much of the local governance of power sharing in the United States is informal, difficult to find and difficult to describe. It could be said that both the formal and informal forms of local governance and power sharing also have a "democratic deficit."

To claim that the comparative importance of professional administration in either the governance of the EU or American local governance constitutes a "democratic deficit" conveys an impoverished understanding of democracy. Democracy is more than political parties, candidates, elections, office holding, law making and revenue setting. Democracy is also the day-to-day operations of governmental agencies and jurisdictions, particularly the processes of interaction between administrative officials and citizens. Professionals engaged in these interactions are as essential to effective democratic government as are elected officials, and local professionals are even more important than elected officials to the give and take of interjurisdictional power sharing.

In their conduct of governance and power sharing, local officials are practicing a form of applied democracy. Consider the literatures upon which the various local government professions are based—city management, law enforcement, fire protection, public works, education, social services. In the case of city and county managers and administrators, the professional treatment of our democratic obligations is highly instructive. The best of this literature points out that local government professionals share policy making responsibilities with elected officials and have formal accountability for responsiveness to community values including efficiency, representation, individual rights, and social equity. According to John Nalbandian, there is a "growing acceptance that the city is a political and social as well as an economic unit and that managers cannot deal with the one without attending to the other. As important as jobs and a growing tax base are for a city, its viability depends as well on its capacity to make collective decisions in a context of growing diversity and interests. In this vein, the tolerance, respect and truthfulness that characterizes among citizens are precious virtues. Government nurtures these virtues as it encourages reflective citizenship—a thoughtful understanding of the citizen's expectations and obligations to the community. It is commonly understood that reflective citizenship cannot be taught; it must be learned by doing. Thus, the process of governance is often government's most important product."

John Nalbandian, in these few words, eloquently answers the "democratic deficit" question. "In short, it is the values and the practices of managers that increasingly will define professionalism in local government, not where city managers work or who hires and fires them. Successful professional managers are and will continue to be those who are able to identify, understand, and work with the values of their community."

Local appointed leaders work for the whole people, for the community near at hand as well as for communities further away. The best local leaders have conceptions of the greater good or the public interest that guide and motivate them, involving a form of morality and a form of faith. Following Harlan Cleveland, the challenges of morality associated with the conduct of multijurisdictional governance are met when "public ethics are in the hearts and minds of individual public executives, and the ultimate court of appeals from their judgments is some surrogate of the people-in-general." Cleveland does not argue that accountability is ultimately to the elected officials of one's jurisdiction. His idea of public responsibility is much bigger than that. To Cleveland the moral responsibilities of public executives include basic considerations of four fundamental principles: "a sense of welfare, a sense of equity, a sense of achievement, and a sense of participating."

Local government administrators live in a world of distant proximities and, according to James Rosenau, the best of them daily navigate "the tensions between core and periphery, between local and national systems, between communitarianism and cosmopolitanism, between cultures and subcultures, between states and markets, between urban and rural, between integration and disintegration, between centralization and decentralization, between universalism and particularism, and between space and pace." They may not be elected, but local government administrators are certainly the foot soldiers of democracy.

Book Eight
Ethics, Fairness and Professionalism in Public Administration

The Atrophy of Ethics

In a word, we are disappointed—disappointed that it was a senior civil servant behind the multi-billion dollar Boeing air tanker scandal. After all, the principals behind other high profile federal scandals—the Ill-Winds defense purchasing scandal, the HUD scandal, the savings and loan scandal, the Fannie Mae scandal—were politically appointed officials. Public administrationist are, of course, disappointed with federal corruption generally, but we have taken some comfort in the fact that it has been they, politically appointed managers, and not we, who have been the culprits. Not this time.

Meet Darlene Druyun, recently the self-described "godmother of the C-17," and now an around-the-clock guest of the federal prison system. She started as a purchasing specialist in NASA and worked her way up to the second most senior Air Force procurement official, overseeing billions of dollars of Air Force contracts. Along the way she became a favorite of the Clinton administration reinventing government crowd for having rigged Air Force numbers, over the objections of her military bosses, to make it appear that the Air Force headcount was smaller than it really was. For this she received a presidential cash bonus. To leave no paper trail she gave verbal orders and twice demoted those who would not sign implicating paperwork. She more or less openly arranged jobs for her daughter and son-in-law with Boeing and finally took a Boeing job herself, where her former Air Force boss, General George Mueller, is now a vice president. But before taking the Boeing job she helped Boeing obtain a grossly inflated $23 billion deal whereby the Pentagon would lease Boeing air tankers rather than buy them and save $5 billion. The Air Force didn't want the lease deal but it was popular on Capitol Hill and, with congressional cover, Ms. Druyun approved it. In her plea bargain she said that she "did favor the Boeing Company in certain negotiations as a result of her employment negotiations and other favors provided by Boeing to the defendant." The Boeing lease deal has been cancelled.

As egregious as the Boeing air tanker scandal was, it is now just another little disappointment floating in a great sea of ethical disappointment. The revolving door of jobs, money, information, and access between the federal government and large contractors swings freely. The Project on Government Oversight estimates that just under 300 former senior government officials have, since 1997, taken top positions in the defense contracting industry or with their lobbyist.

Looking out across the great sea of ethical disappointment one sees the torture of prisoners; the general melt-down of the public accounting business, the business that is supposed to protect the interests of corporate stock holders; the relentless accumulation of corporate scandals—Enron, WorldCom, Tyco, Westar, Freddy Mac, Fannie Mae; governmental funds for policy propaganda, including bribes to so-called reporters; an electoral system that cannot be trusted; a legislative electoral system grossly tilted in favor of incumbents; and so much money in politics that the old joke that we have the best government money can but is no longer a joke.

Why do corporate corruption and government corruption seem so ordinary and commonplace? Are our moral muscles so lacking in exercise that they have begun to atrophy? Are we so hardened to ethical disappointment that we can no longer be outraged? Are we so shameless that we are reluctant to find shame in others? The economist and philosopher Albert O. Hirschman, in *Shifting Involvements: Private Interests and Public Action,* thinks so: "In this manner, corruption, which is at first a response to dissatisfaction with public affairs becomes a determinant of further, more profound disaffection, which in turn sets the stage for more corruption. At the end of the process the public spirit is driven out altogether."

The reform architecture of the American Progressive Era, including merit-based civil service system at all levels of government as well as the creation of instruments for the firm regulation of business, was an expression of our disappointment with late nineteenth and early twentieth century government corruption and corporate excess. But by the mid-twentieth century, disappointment with large, slow, unresponsive government bureaucracies and with what many believed to be excessive control of business, begun to register. The deregulation of business came into fashion, as did cutting back the civil service and contracting-out much of government work. In a cumulative dynamic from that time until this, we now find ourselves in a state of "unblushing confusion of the business of government with the promotion of private fortune." And we are once again disappointed. At what point will our collective disappointment trigger a steady oscillation back toward public regard?

We are, I believe, at that tipping point. However the steady reintroduction of public affairs and public ethics into American life will require imagination, constructive bridges between public problems and public institutions, and the invention of a new public language. Because the world is greatly changed, we cannot simply return to the way things used to be. We will not put Humpty Dumpty together again.

At the risk of a vast oversimplification, I believe that the elements necessary to tip American affairs toward an effective public sector and a vital public ethics are these:

First, governmental contracting-out is here to stay—it is the means by which Americans can have both the illusion of smaller government with no diminution in government services. In view of this, there must be an infusion of public morality among primary government contractors and the development of a language of public service, efficiency, fairness, and service in government-contractor relationships. In addition to Donald Kettl's call for government to be a smarter buyer, I suggest that governments set the example by contracting only with non-profits and firms with records of transparency and honesty. Our breach of the revolving door or any attempt to influence contract relations should result in disqualification from *all* government contracts.

173

Second, public ethics would be strengthened if the line between politics and administration were brighter. (Yes, I know that many readers believe the politics-administration dichotomy to be dead. I do not.) Under current circumstances the neutrality, expertise, and objectivity of merit-protected civil servants is very badly needed to hold the line against the excesses of politics. Consider the examples of military base closings, the conduct of the census, and the annual pork barrel spending embarrassment. In these and other cases, an infusion of good old fashioned public administration would go a long way toward perception of integrity to government. A positive step right now would be for states to put in place systems of election management that are professional and neutral. Nothing would do more to restore our trust in elections.

Third, in the face of increasing jurisdictional fragmentation on the one hand and social, economic, and political problems that do not march jurisdictional lines on the other hand, it is difficult to ground governmental and corporate ethics entirely on law. There are simply too many layers of laws, and laws still do not carry themselves out. So we rely on the public-service profession and on educational processes that lead to the professions to serve as the foundation of our ethics, as the standard setters and the standard enforcers, and as the places where we discuss and debate ethics issues.

Finally, the highest of public service ethics can require courage. Public administrators should be openly and vocally in support of our colleagues who are speaking truth to power, are standing for openness and transparency, and are blowing the whistle on corruption. Public administrators should be prepared to stand up to and root out the corrupt among us.

What about Evil?

"Evil" is certainly among the most powerful and evocative words in contemporary public discourse. There was once an empire of evil and now there is an axis of evil. Evil regimes and leaders are abroad in the world—dangerous, threatening, dark, and mysterious. There is

174

evil among us and some of it, we are told, is administrative, administrative evil needing to be unmasked. Evil and its opposite, good, are, it is said, dichotomous categories into which individuals and their actions, groups and their actions, ideologies, and even cultures can be reliably placed.

Among the more useful considerations of evil is the description of it by Gandhi. He, too, used dichotomous categories to describe good and evil but rather than characterizing particular leaders, their regimes or their policies as evil, he found evil to be well within each individual's capacity to both understand and act on. He had good reason to characterize the particular leaders, regimes and actions of his time as evil, but he chose instead to set out an understanding of evil that is abstract and therefore particularly useful and enduring. In his description Gandhi did not include those evils so obvious and fundamental to human understanding that they did not require elaboration, such as involuntary servitude or the taking of innocent life. An abstract and even philosophical approach to evil on the part of a political leader was unusual in Gandhi's time and would be even more unusual today, when the word "evil" is so frequently and casually used. Here, in summary form and with a few minor changes to put them into our present context, is Gandhi's description of the forms of evil.

Poverty amid plenty is evil, and those policies and actions that consciously favor the interests of those with plenty at the expense of those in poverty are likewise evil. Virtually all forms of theology teach us that those with resources have responsibilities toward those without resources. Persons and groups of persons who have plenty have responsibilities toward those who do not and well-off nations have responsibilities toward less well-off nations. Nothing, not race, not gender, not ideology, not geography, can mitigate the evil of those with plenty ignoring the needs of those with little. The reason the concept of social equity has such resonance, as a core ethic in American public administration is that we instinctively recognize the evil of poverty amid plenty.

Wealth without work is evil. Because the poor in our uneven world usually work tirelessly just to survive, it is evil for those with plenty to be idle. Remember the little rhyme by Sarah Gleghorn (1915) that so profoundly captured the evil of wealth without work that it influenced the development of much stronger British and American child labor laws:

The golf links lie so near the mill
That almost any day
The laboring children can look out
And see the men at play.

Although there has been progress in many parts of the world, the challenges of child labor and human exploitation are no less now than they were in Gandhi's time. Our wealth is easily seen by others, but it is not easy for us to see their privation.

Commerce without morality can be evil. In most respects the modern corporation and its operation in the capitalist marketplace is a positive force for good in the world, forming the base of gainful work for millions while improving products and providing services. But the exploitation of both humankind and our environment for commercial gain is far too evident in the world and is a great evil.

Science and technology without humanity can be evil. Science gives us better food, better health, and longer lives. Technology can reduce human toil and greatly enhance human communication and knowledge. Science and technology can be instruments for a more humane world. But when the benefits of science and technology are so unevenly distributed around the world or when science and technology are used for inhumane purposes they are evil. The moral implications of nuclear wars on one hand and suicide bombers on the other are clear. Modern science and technology both bless us and cause us to face potential evils never before faced by humankind.

The practices of politics and administration without principles can be evil. In his time Gandhi was probably most concerned with the evils associated with European policies of empire and their implementation in India. In our time we face the challenges of political and administrative evil in Iraq, for example the evil of Saddam Hussein on one hand and prisoner abuse on the other. We should never tire of asking these questions: What exactly are our political and administrative principles, and do we believe them to be good? For whom are our principles good? Do current policies or proposed policies further those principles? How can policies thought to be favorably associated with our principles be implemented without doing evil?

Knowledge without character can be evil. Although we live, it is said, in a knowledge society, knowledge never has been synonymous with either wisdom or character. One way to ensure greater character in the application of knowledge to human affairs is to do all that can be done to make knowledge widely available and to demand transparency. Knowledge comes in many forms and in the hierarchies of knowledge, local knowledge tends to be discounted. This is nonsense because all knowledge when applied must be applied locally. It is at the local level where policy is carried out that character is most likely to meet knowledge and ideas passing for knowledge. Consider, for example, local school districts. It would seem that local school officials do not know as much about schooling as do expert policy makers and politicians at the state and national level. It requires little character to push knowledge-based arguments that one is not asked to carry out. The denial of local knowledge reduces the prospects of bringing real character to policy implementation at the level where it matters most.

Knowledge based on technical expertise is vital but so too is local knowledge based on culture, tradition, and context. Effective politics and administration very often involve carefully built patterns of accommodation between technical expertise and local knowledge.

Promiscuous use of the word "evil" in contemporary political discourse drains it of meaning and does little to advance a generalized good. Without doubt there is evil in the world. Gandhi teaches us that the evil that matters most and the evil we are likely to be able to influence is near at hand. It is the evil of poverty amid plenty, wealth without work, commerce without morality, politics and administration without principles, science and technology without morality and knowledge without character. If we individually and collectively face down these evils the world would be a better place.

Public Administration and Social Equity

In the late 1960s, when my original essay on social equity in public administration was published in Frank Marini's book *Toward a New Public Administration*, there was war abroad and social turbulence at home. At the heart of the challenges facing public administration were very serious questions of fairness. Minorities and the children of the poor were dying in disproportionate numbers in Viet Nam. Several of our great cities were torn apart by riots. In the South civil rights marchers were demanding full voting rights and equal access to public services and facilities. At the time many were impressed by how much public administration had to say about better management and organizational efficiency and economy, and how little it had to say about matters of fundamental fairness and justice. It was clear that greater efficiency and economy were not going to solve the problems the U.S. faced at the time. It was in this context that social equity in public administration was born.

Social equity in public administration has a particularly impressive provenance. After all, in his 1887 founding essay Woodrow Wilson wrote that in the past, "the question was always: Who shall make the law, and what shall the law be?" Then Wilson turned to the new question: "How shall the law be administered with enlightenment, with equity, with speed, and without friction?" To be sure, in the years that followed, public administration largely ignored equity and gave its attention to efficiency, economy, and friction-reducing organizational arrangements. But, in the late 1960s, we were face-to-face with Wilson's question: "How shall the law be administered with enlightenment, with equity?"

Over the years social equity has taken its place in public administration as a unique body of concepts and principles that attempt to answer Wilson's question. The scope of social equity has expanded to consider whether and how the field might combat organizational and policy factors that contribute to inequality. In the past 30 years, these concepts and principles have importantly influenced both the theory and

178

the practice of public administration and have challenged the field to come to terms with its obligation to deal with fundamental questions of fairness. But, as America enters the 21st century, public administration faces particularly pressing social equity challenges.

Among many Americans there is now a strongly held belief that things are simply not fair. The booming economy of the 1990s, combined with extensive deregulation of business, has brought with it a growing gap between the haves and the have nots. The wealth of the top 5 percent of U.S. households exceeds the combined financial wealth of the remaining 95 percent, and the top 20 percent of American households has 50 percent of the wealth while the bottom 20 percent has less than 4 percent.

A recent report from the Department of Health and Human Services indicates that while there has been significant overall improvement in the health status of Americans, "not all groups have benefited equally, and substantial differences between racial/ethnic groups persist." Furthermore, the gap between those with adequate health insurance and those without out it is widening, particularly for the so-called working poor. The question is not whether we have the best health care in the world, because we do. The question is, health care for whom?

Among democratic and developed countries, the United States has the highest percentage of its population in jail or prison and minorities are disproportionately represented in the prison population. The federalization of crime in America continues, with the federal prison system growing the most rapidly. Just over 60 percent of federal prisoners are there on drug convictions, again disproportionately minority.

This review of the widening gap between the haves and have nots could go on and on, but the point is made—the reason so many Americans think that things are not fair is because they are not.

What, you might ask, does this have to do with public administration? Nothing if we adhere to the position that policy is distinct from administration and that administration should be passive about and disinterested in policy. We just do what the law and our superiors tell us to do. It has everything to do with it if we understand the practice of public administration to involve advice and influence on policy. It has everything to do with it if we recognize that public administrators have a range of discretion in the implementation of policy and that the exercise of that discretion is a particularly important form of policy making. And we regard exclusion from policy to be both impossible and undesirable. Virtually all of the modern theory and practice of public administration recognizes the policy responsibilities of public administration.

But what can we do about the widening gap between the haves and the have nots? First, as leaders and advisors on policy, we can speak out, particularly in the areas of our expertise. This does not necessarily mean shouting publicly about unfair policy, although there may be times when that is called for. But it does mean speaking truth to power in the corridors of policy making. Second, within the range of our discretion we can work diligently to mitigate the unfair consequences of policy. Third, we can give to issues of fairness the same creativity and attention we give to measuring performance and being efficient. Finally, we have always been able to promote process equity—equal access and opportunity, equal treatment and protection, and due process—and work is constantly needed to achieve it in every agency at all levels of government.

As a core value in public administration, social equity is no longer novel or new. Social equity is in many ways at middle age, experiencing the advantages of some maturity and general acceptance. But much has changed since the formal inclusion of social equity in the pantheon of public administration values in the 1970s. These changes could be summed up in this irony—in the past thirty years social equity has grown in importance in public administration at the same time that in virtually all aspects of social, economic, and political life, Americans have become less equal. In our literature, in our classrooms, and in our administrative practices we have learned the language of social equity. But, if the data on the growing gap between the haves and have nots in American are any indication, we are not walking the social equity talk.

There is little doubt that inequality in America would be worse were it not for public administrators dedicated to social equity in their practices. And there is no question that the broader contexts of

American politics have tilted the playing field toward the advantaged and away from the disadvantaged, making contemporary commitments on the part of public administrators to social equity particularly difficult. Walking the social equity talk in our time is not only difficult it may be dangerous to one's career.

While we have been promoting democracy abroad and even fighting to bring democracy to others, democracy at home is in trouble. The recent report of the Task Force on Inequality in America of the American Political Science Association puts it this way: "Our country's ideals of equal citizenship and responsive government may be under growing threat in an era of persistent and rising inequality. Disparities of income, wealth, and access to opportunity are growing more sharply in the United States than in many other nations, and gaps between races and ethnic groups persist. Progress toward realizing American ideals of democracy may have stalled, and in some arenas reversed."

In the manner of political science, the APSA Task Force Report calls for research on matters of social equity and for "the engagement of political science with improving American democracy through scholarship." For two reasons those identified with public administration, either as a field of political science or a free standing academic field and a body of professional practice, are inclined to a less passive and more engaged approach to the problems of inequality in America. First, the argument that policy and politics are on one side of a dichotomy and public administration is on the other and those issues of inequality belong on the politics and policy side of the dichotomy and not on the public administration side must be rejected. Virtually all empirical research in the field indicates that public administration is highly influential in policy making and makes policy in all of the processes of policy implementation. I insist that public administration cannot hide behind the dichotomy in the matter of social equity. Second, as an academic field, a body of research and a field of professional practice, public administration has always been applied. After all how can we run the Constitution and carry out the laws if we do not get our hands dirty? But for public administration I insist that we *engage* inequality, that we dirty our hands with inequality, that we be outraged, passionate, and determined. In short, I insist that we actually apply social equity in public administration, and here is an agenda for that project.

First, like our environmental friends, when it comes to social equity we should think globally and act locally. Indeed all important matters of social equity are local, local in the sense of consequences. The results of national policies are all manifested locally, in our neighborhoods, in our families, in our cities and in our workplaces.

Second, it is time to be engaged in the war of ideas. Public administration people are, after all, still citizens. It is time for public administrators of all kinds to relentlessly ask the so-called second question. The first question is whether an existing public program or a proposed program is effective or good (or bad). The second question is more important. *For whom is this program effective or good?* Ignore those who reply to the second question with the charge that those who ask the second question are practicing class warfare. Answer the class warfare charge immediately with the point that you will not ask the second question, *for whom is this program effective or good,* if those who allege a program to be good or bad can demonstrate that it is universally good or bad. If that doesn't work try this retort. *You say that I am practicing class warfare. Nonsense. I am engaged in the war of ideas and my idea is fair and yours is not. Stop tossing around class warfare slogans and engage me in the war of ideas.*

Third, it is important to remember that it isn't necessarily good ideas that win the war of ideas. Indeed, many rather bad ideas have won the war of ideas recently. When there is determination, organization, money, and persistence behind an idea it will likely win the war. Because public administrationists know how to organize, and are determined and persistent, we are natural social equity warriors.

Fourth, like it or not, senior public administrators and those of us who study public administration are part of the elite, the privileged. There is a distinct patronizing tone to social equity in much of our literature and ideology. A commitment to social equity obliges us to see after the interests of those who are denied opportunities or are disadvantaged regardless of their competence. At the intermediate and upper levels of public administration we tend to avoid the uncomfortable issue of competence, although street-level workers have no illusions about competence.

There are interesting lessons on this subject. One is the lesson and life of Gandhi who insisted on the collective non-violent expression of demands for fairness on the part of the least advantaged acting together. Another is the lesson of the Roundheads, citizens below the elite who asserted a belief in the individual, independent of class, insisted on egalitarian politics and were suspicious of elites in their hierarchical polity. The American founding was a denial of aristocracy a triumph of Roundhead reasoning. In much of social equity there is democratic rhetoric but aristocratic assumptions. We search still for versions of social equity in public administration that enables the disadvantaged without attempts to lead them.

Fifth, it is high time for moral indignation, for passion and anger. The moral high ground, often put passionately as Christian doctrine, has tended toward those interested in issues such as abortion, gay marriage, human cloning, stem-cell research, and euthanasia, and those mobilized in pursuit of these issues have proven to be formidable. Issues of poverty, at least from the biblical Christian perspective, are far more central to doctrine than the issues mentioned above. But, it is far more difficult to bring indignation and passion to matters of poverty. Still, that is what needs to be done.

To stir an interest in social equity we should consider alternative methodologies and medias of presentation. Consider, for example, the statistics regarding the grossly disproportionate percentage of African Americans who are in prison. We know those appalling statistics forward and backwards and it seems to make little difference. Stories, films, videos, novels, essays, plays, and personal descriptions of the ravages of overly long sentences for drug offenses have the power to move people and also to move policy makers. Stories of single mothers working two jobs and still falling behind are compelling, for example, and hold some prospects for moving readers and viewers. There is a desperate need to dramatize social equity issues, to bring them to life. We need modern equivalents of *The Grapes of Wrath.* I am convinced that if the general population understood more fully the effects of discrimination and poverty on American lives they would respond by supporting political candidates committed to social equity. Politics is all about winning and majority rule. Public administration should be all about seeing to it that public policies are fair and that the implementation of public policies is fair. We are long past needing to defend this proposition. It is time to walk the social equity talk.

By doing these five things we can respond to Woodrow Wilson's description of our field as the administration of the law with enlightenment and equity.

Is Social Equity Class Warfare?

During a session on social equity at a national public administration conference, I was startled to hear one of the participants describe social equity as class warfare. In a time of national crisis, the speaker said, we should be united, and it is inappropriate for people in public administration to emphasize our differences and divide us. It is not the place of public administration to concern itself with matters of fairness and equity between, as he put it, the classes. The class warfare comment dissolved the session into a rhetorical and ideological shouting match, destroying any hope of reasoned deliberation. I was too stunned to react, and the moment passed. But, from that moment to this, like a splinter, the argument that the pursuit of social equity in public administration is a form of class warfare has nagged at me. Please join me as I pull that splinter out.

My first unspoken reaction was this: If social equity in public administration is class warfare, sign me up and give me a uniform. This is a war worth fighting. Obviously this response indicated that I was as drunk on the rhetoric of social equity as the speaker was on the rhetoric of class warfare. Gradually I sobered up.

My second reaction was befitting my line of work. I wondered, like any professor would, if there was something I had missed, something new and profound in either the field of public administration or the circumstances and conditions in which Americans live. When professors have doubts about what they think they know, they retreat to the research and literature on the subject in question. This is what I found.

The two best recent studies of social and economic circumstances in the United States are Lisa A. Keister's *Wealth in America: Trends in Wealth Inequality,* published in 2000, and Kevin Phillips popular *Wealth and Democracy*. Both studies bring together an impressive array of information over an extended period of time, sufficient to give informed historical perspective to the subject. Both insist on the importance of distinguishing between wealth and intergenerational wealth accumulation on one hand and annual income on the other hand. Regarding the contemporary accumulation of wealth, both studies find that in the whole sweep of American history there has never been greater concentration of wealth in the hands of the few. Even the concentration of wealth in the hands of the robber barons of the late nineteenth century Gilded Age does not surpass the present percentages of American wealth in the hands of the few. By the year 2000, the top one percent of the population controlled 40 percent of the wealth, and the top 20 percent controlled a staggering 93 percent of American financial wealth. For the past 20 years the gap between those who have significant financial wealth and those who do not has grown steadily wider. While the details are somewhat different, the gap between the annual income of the top five percent of Americans and the bottom 60 percent has also grown steadily. For the past 35 years the after-tax net income adjusted for inflation of the bottom 80 percent of Americans has stayed essentially the same, but for the richest six percent it has more than tripled. Wealth and income inequality are closely correlated with race and gender; African-Americans, Hispanic-Americans, and working mothers are significantly over-represented among the poor. Annually the top one-fifth make 11 times more than those in the bottom fifth, by far the widest gap among the industrialized democracies.

Compared to 30 years ago, American wage earners have smaller pensions, less health insurance coverage, much greater non-mortgage consumer debt, and considerably less job security. Longer working hours, longer commutes and two-earner families buffet wage earners, and the overall indices of American social health have been in decline for years. These two excellent books provide conclusive evidence that there really is serious social inequality in the United States.

What, the astute reader will ask, does this have to do with public administration? Let me count the ways. First, there is a very close association between wealth and income on one hand and political influence and governmental policy on the other. For example, corporate income, capital gains and inheritance taxes have all been sharply cut as income and wealth disparity has increased. Second, inequality expresses itself, often powerfully, in all of the fields of public policy—education, transportation, public safety, child welfare, the environment, agriculture, natural resources, national defense and so forth. Because public administrators implement these public policies, as inequality and unfairness are increasingly evident, we are faced with social equity problems. It is government, not the market, that is set up to deal with issues of fairness and justice. Can public administrators simply say Kings X; issues of fairness and justice are political and not administrative? I don't think so. Third, it is everywhere evident that a child's early conditions and circumstances, to a considerable extent, determine that child's chances in life. We do not start the race of life evenly. So long as income and wealth disparities are increasing, growing percentages of American children face the prospects of diminished life prospects. If we are asked to implement the policies that systematically advantage a few at the expense of the many, do we not have social equity responsibilities?

I think we do.

It is interesting to remember that the growth of modern American public administration was closely associated with the Progressive Era, with stamping out government political corruption, and with curbing the excesses of corporations and the wealthy. Social equity has a long and honorable provenance in public administration.

To return to the question: Is social equity in public administration a form of class warfare? To uncover and describe inequity and unfairness is not class warfare; it is simply enlightened transparency in government. It is, after all, variations in wealth and income that divide us, not descriptions of wealth and income. To do what one can within the constraints of law and policy to implement policy in a way that is fair and just is not class warfare; it is simply good public administration. To seek to change law or policy that is unfair or inequitable is not class warfare; it is part of our moral responsibility. To be an informed and expert voice for fairness and equity in the processes of policy formulation is not class warfare; it is part of the public administrator's job description.

Ethics and Contracting-Out

As we move inexorably toward third party government, both the theory and practice of public administration are changing. Fewer and fewer of those who actually administer or direct public services are civil servants. Paul Light's estimate in *The True Size of Government* is that there are more than eight full-time equivalent federal contract and grant employees for every one direct government employee. Some federal agencies are now so hollowed-out that their sole function is to oversee the grants and contracts being implemented by the non-profit and for-profit organizations that do the agencies work. To give you an idea of the dimensions of third party government, consider the Centers for Medicare and Medicaid (CMS) of the Department of Health and Human Services. If one includes the state contributions to Medicaid, the total annual budget of CMS is nearly 500 billion dollars. The staff of CMS is about 4,500 people; therefore for every one CMS employee, there are over five million dollars of federal and state expenditures. Now *that* is hollowed out. In the face of third party government the field is faced with the need to redefine exactly what public administration means.

In the interest of a dialogue let me suggest the following adjustment to our definition of what we believe public administration to be.

First, we must insist that the word "public" in public administration does not mean the same thing as government. The founders of the field wisely called it public rather than governmental administration recognizing that public administration includes direct government administration and related public activities such as utilities, the regulation of commerce and the work of government contract and grant holders.

Second, we should borrow a splendid idea from administrative law and change it from a legal idea to part of the philosophical and moral basis of modern public administration. That idea goes variously by the following phrases: "clothed with the public interest," "covered with a public purpose," or "affected with a public interest." In the law, all of these phrases are intended to describe what ought properly to be thought of as "state action." In an excellent and under-appreciated article in *Public Administration Review,* Robert S. Gilmour and Laura S. Jensen reviewed the state of the law regarding whether public functions delegated by contract or grant to private actors are nevertheless still public functions and a form of state action. Put another way and in the form of a question: "When public functions are delegated to private actors and are allowed to be transformed to private actions, is public accountability inevitably lost?" As you might expect, Gilmour and Jensen find the state of the law on this matter fuzzy and unsettled. While the state of the law is important to contract managers, a too narrow focus on the law might obscure the potential of the core idea.

Third, we have in the logic of extended state action covered with a public purpose a compelling and powerful basis upon which to define public administration in the era of third party government. It is incorrect to claim that the employees The Corrections Corporation of America (contract prison operators) or The Kaiser Group (healthcare providers) are civil servants, but it is certainly correct to claim that when their employees are implementing a government contract paid for by taxpayer money, their work constitutes the extended action of the state and that that work is covered with a public purpose.

Fourth, in the context of American separation of powers, elected officials delegate, ordinarily to the executive branch, the power to act for the state. When the power to act for the state is in turn extended by grant or contract to either non-profit or corporate institutions, those institutions engage in state action and that state action is, by definition, covered with a public purpose. Public agencies and their officials should build into contracts and grants the expectation of extended state action covered with a public purpose. This should not be primarily for purposes of accountability in case things go wrong; that has for too long been the focus of the law. Instead, agencies and officials should work with contractors to recognize that they are part of the extended management of the agency and that in the implementation of contracts that they, like public officials, act as agents of the state and are expected to fulfill public purposes. In a contract sense extended state action might be thought of as formal and legal obligations on the part of contractors, but in a larger sense, and as a fundamental norm, contractors should see themselves as engaged in extended state action covered with a public purpose. This philosophy should be part of the whole foundation of public administration, the foundation upon which the logic of contracting rests.

Fifth, such an approach to public administration in the era of third party government will require an extensive reworking of our primary theories. The works of Donald Kettl, Lester Salamon, Brinton Milward, Philip Cooper, Ronald Moe, Barry Bozeman, Robert Gilmour, Laura Jensen, Ruth DeHoog, Pauline Rosenau, and others are a very good start. Our textbooks need to be rewritten. Our MPA degrees need to be reoriented. We should organize extensive training regimes that combine governmental and contract officials in their shared responsibilities to manage contracts for public purposes.

Some will argued that this definition of public administration is too broad, too grand. They will also argue that such an approach to public administration is impractical. I disagree. In practical terms the era of third party government is already here and public administration is trying to catch up. The nostrums of reinventing government, while advocating steering rather than rowing and outcomes rather than inputs, are of little help normatively because they were too focused on just one public purpose—efficiency. The norms of extended state action covered with public purposes are much more broad than efficiency and include responsiveness, compassion, social equity, and justice. When contractors think that their sole purpose is to deliver public services efficiently for the least cost, they have it only partly right. It is also their primary obligation to be fair, responsive to changing circumstances not anticipated in contracts, evenhanded, and just. If contractors act as agents of the state they must learn that their obligations go beyond contract law and include, indeed embrace, the norms of extended state action covered with public purposes. In the long run, unless this happens, democracies will turn away from third party government.

Ethics, Contracting-Out, and Qui Tam?

The dusty halls of constitutional and administrative law are a dangerous and mysterious place, especially to the bureaucrat. Severely dressed lawyers gather there, mostly it seems, for the purpose of finding reasons why good public administrators cannot do the efficient thing or, worse yet, the right thing. It is tough to be a leader, an entrepreneur, a risk taker, and an institution builder, when weighed down by libraries filled with laws and battalions of lawyers armed with those laws. Still, we bureaucrats carry out the law as best we can.

But now comes an ancient and wonderful thing from the law, a thing which will lift our spirits, improve our work, and remind us of the good we inherit from bureaucrats past. This thing is qui tam.

Qui tam you ask? Yes, I answer, qui tam, which is pronounced *key tam*. Now, at the risk of a sharp rebuke from my administrative law friends for wandering into their dusty halls without a license, I will do my best to explain qui tam.

During the Civil War, one of the biggest problems on the Union side was the persistence of fraud by contractors against the government. So, based on the advice of good bureaucrats and government lawyers, Congress passed, and President Lincoln signed, the False Claims Act (FSC) (31 U.S.C. Sections 3729-33) of 1863. The FSC allows private citizens with knowledge of prior or present fraud committed against the federal government by contractors to bring suit against those contractors, on behalf of the government. Based on such suits the federal government can recover compensatory damages based on stiff penalties as high as triple damages, against fraudulent contractors. But that isn't all. The original private citizen bringing the suit joins the government in the receipt of the damages to the tune of as much as 25 percent. Qui tam is short for a longer Latin phrase which means approximately, "one who brings an action for the king as well as for one's self." The False Claims Act of 1863 is based on the logic of qui tam and assumes that there is good to be found in the citizen who will report wrongdoing and that both the government representing all the people, as well as that good citizen can share in rewards. Now *that* is real citizen participation!

The citizen bringing suit under qui tam is known in the False Claims Act as the "relator," not the informer or the whistle blower. As is so often the case, those who came before us were better at English than we are. Relator is a dignified word, a word without ideological baggage. Informer and whistle blower are, by comparison, dreadful words. So, I propose that we refer to all of those reporting fraud as relators. After all, Abraham Lincoln signed the law.

Over the years there have been about 2,500 qui tam suits, which have recovered about $1 billion of fraud. These days the big qui tam action is in Medicare fraud. A suit that recently worked its way up the appellate system was brought by Donald Steven McLendon who alleged that Columbia/HCA used inflated management fees and other rigged expenses, reimbursed by Medicare, to purchase home health care agencies, marketing, and executive perks. "The government was really funding Columbia's acquisitions," said McLendon's attorney, Marlan Wilbanks of Harmon, Smith, Bridges & Wilbanks of Atlanta. "We believe we have identified hundreds of millions of dollars of fraud." Based on a judgment in favor of McLendon, the case was settled at $745 million, a portion of which goes to him.

Another compelling feature of qui tam has to do with fiscal federalism. It turns out that when federal money is passed to the states and municipalities, and they then act as the agents for spending that money by contract, the contractors are subject to the qui tam provisions of the False Claims Act. So, state and local contractors for a wide range of services such as elder care, welfare to work training and job search, drug and alcohol rehabilitation, foster care for children, and the like, are subject to qui tam. Because federal dollars fund, in whole or in part, these contracted services, fraudulent contractors can be qui tammed.

If there is a contemporary public management passion it is contracting out. We seem to have forgotten that the most serious problems of government corruption have always had to do with financial dealings between government and non-governmental organizations and individuals. That was what the HUD scandal was about. That is what the Ill Winds scandal was all about. And, to some extent, that is what the S&L scandal was all about. As contracting flourishes, the opportunities and possibilities for fraudulent action also flourish. We have probably been quicker to embrace contracting than we have been to set up the safeguards to protect us from contracting fraud. Indeed, we have been going the other way, with deregulation, and increased agency discretion to improve efficiency.

The contractor tempted to skim the contract or use contract funds to remodel the kitchen, would want to know about qui tam and thus knowing, might think twice. We are still left with the moral question of organizational loyalty and the snitch. My reading of the contemporary public administration ethics literature suggests that ethics is both an organizational and a personal responsibility. That being so, would it not be unethical for a public official knowing of fraud and unable to correct it inside the fraudulent organization, to fail to act on the outside? Is a qui tam action not an affirmative exercise of ethics?

The broader literature of our field has redefined public administration from just government administration to the administration of public serving activities in governmental, nonprofit, contracting, and other paragovernmental settings. Therefore, is the employee of a fraudulent contracting company not also a public official, a part of the great shadow bureaucracy? I believe the answer to be yes. If it is yes, does that official have a duty to act? Yes again. Is qui tam an appropriate form of action, when other forms of action have failed? Yes again. Do we not teach that the good public official must also be a good citizen, a representative citizen? Is there anything wrong with financial incentives to good citizenship, particularly in the face of the threats toward those who uncover fraud?

James Alderson, was the former chief financial officer of a Montana hospital run by a company once owned by HCA, Inc., the nation's largest for-profit hospital chain. Alderson was fired for refusing to file cost reports he knew to be false, reports that formed the basis of the hospital's claims for Medicare reimbursement. It turns out that the company running the hospital was keeping a secret set of books that detailed reimbursement claims based on cost reports that were false. Alderson filed a lawsuit against the company under the provisions of the False Claims Act.

Robert Rothfeder and Dennis Wyman, were both independent contractors who worked as staff emergency physicians at Lakeview Hospital in West Valley City, Utah. Lakeview was a wholly owned subsidiary of HealthTrust, which later merged with what is now HCA, Inc. Wyman and Rothfeder have over 20 years of experience as emergency room physicians and Wyman was once named Utah's emergency medical services physician of the year. Rothfeder serves on the board of the Utah chapter of the American College of Emergency Physicians. It turns out that each time Wyman and Rothfeder ordered a basic blood test or a basic chemistry profile for a patient, the hospital ordered various additional blood and chemistry tests. When Wyman questioned the hospital manager about this practice he was told that these additional tests did not result in additional costs to patients, to Medicare, or to other insurers. Because they were suspicious of fraud on the part of the hospital, Wyman and Rothfeder, like James Alderson, filed suit against the hospital under the provisions of the False Claims Act of 1863.

John Schilling was a former reimbursement manager for Olsten's, a home health services company in Florida. Shilling discovered that wildly inflated management fees were being passed on to Medicare

Public Administration with an Attitude

through the company's cost reports. After the company refused to submit realistic management fees he brought suit. And this is James Thompson, a Texas physician who refused to file false claims and take kickbacks from hospitals for having referred Medicare and Medicaid patients to their facilities. Because of this, other physicians who were taking kickbacks forced him to work alone because they refused to share on-call duties. So Thompson also brought suit.

Shilling, Thompson, and the others you have just met have these things in common. First, they are not public servants in a formal and technical sense; they are instead employees of nonprofit or for-profit organizations doing the public's work by contract. They are part of that great shadow bureaucracy now estimated at more than eight contract bureaucrats for every one actual bureaucrat, a reinventing government advocate's dream come true. Second, they understand fraud, kickbacks, and contract skimming as readily and as clearly as any ordinary public official does. Third, at considerable risk to themselves professionally or to their companies, they had the courage to take fraudulent companies to court.

HCA, Inc. has paid a $631 million settlement for having systematically overcharged Medicare and other public insurance programs. Subject to approval by the Justice Department, this settlement comes on the heels of a 2000 settlement of $840 million for the same thing, including kickbacks to doctors. As a part of these settlements, Alderson, Rothfeder and Wyman, Thompson, Schilling, and others share part of the recovered damages. The Department of Justice reports that civil fraud recoveries are now averaging over $1 billion annually, most of the recoveries based on qui tam lawsuits brought against companies found to have defrauded the government. Health care fraud is the largest field of fraud recovery followed by recoveries involving the production of oil and other minerals from public lands (in the year 2000 alone, $95 million from Chevron, $56 million from Shell, $43 million from Texaco, $32 million from BPAmoco, $26 million from Conoco, and $12 million from Devon Energy. These settlements were all the result of a qui tam lawsuit against 14 oil companies filed in 1996 by J. Benjamin Johnson

194

and John Martinek, former employees of Atlantic Richfield Co.)

In 2000 there were $140 million in fraud recoveries from brokerage firms. Imagine what this is going to be in the future given the accounting firm and brokerage house scandals. Finally, defense procurement fraud recoveries for 2000 were just over $100 million.

Senator Charles E. Grassley (R-Iowa) is the living patron saint of the False Claims Act and of the provisions of qui tam. But Senator Grassley, shortly before being named Chair of the Senate Finance Committee, was not happy with the results of these settlements. In a statement released shortly after the announcement of the proposed settlement between HCA, Inc., and the Department of Justice, Senator Grassley indicated that he was appalled to think that the government would settle for such a small amount, given the magnitude of the HCA fraud.

Some will be concerned that the logic of qui tam allows private citizens and public servants to bring a legal action both for the government and for themselves. The purist will argue that neither the civil servant nor the third-party public administrator should enrich themselves simply for having done their duty. I might be inclined to agree if it were not for the fact that the corps of modern day federal contract managers is woefully undertrained and understaffed, conditions that virtually invite fraud. At least the False Claims Act and qui tam is there to give pause to those considering contract fraud.

We are still left with the moral question of whether a public official should enrich himself or herself by doing good. My favorite version of this is the whine by a group of California attorneys to the effect that it is wrong for public officials to get rich by protecting the public through qui tam. Hmmm ... and this is coming from lawyers?

Arthur Andersen, Where Art Thou?

As an undergraduate majoring in political science back in the twentieth century, my advisor pointed out that the study of government seldom led to promising career prospects. He recommended that I minor in accounting because there were jobs and because, he said, accounting suited my personality. In pursuit of this minor I found a powerful almost genetic connection between accounting and public administration. The core purpose of accounting is, after all, to verify, to authenticate, to certify to the public the integrity of the accounts of a business or a public agency. It is through the external and independent auditing process that the public can know whether a company is or is not profitable or whether taxpayer money is properly spent. Standing at the center of the field was the great Arthur Andersen, the Dwight Waldo or Herbert Simon of accounting. The stock answer to the most vexing accounting question was another question—what would Arthur Andersen do? Andersen, and the firm he built, was the embodiment of public accounting independence, courage, and integrity. A favorable annual audit by the Arthur Andersen Company or one of the other Big Eight (later the Big Six and now the Final Four) accounting firms was the badge of approval, the coin of the realm. How could things have gone so terribly wrong?

To answer this question, let me recount an experience. Some years ago I was responsible for a public university in the state of Washington. At the end of my first year there, the report of the mandatory annual audit by one of the Big Eight accounting firms arrived and I read it with interest and amazement. After a few pages of tabular material and balance sheets, there were at least 25 pages of management letter comments, most of them highly critical of the management of the university. Buried in the criticism of management was the essential operative phrase for which I was looking—the books of the university were in balance and all public monies were properly accounted for.

Knowing that this audit report was going to be seen by several powerful political and administrative officials in the state capital, I was deeply concerned about all of the criticism of the university management. So I set up a lunch with the primary local representative of the auditing firm. He showed up with a very young partner, whom I assumed to be another certified public accountant. After the preliminaries, I asked him how a financial audit of the university became a critique of university management. After some comments about the lack of accounting controls and what he believed to be weak information technology capacity at the university, he deferred to his partner who turned out to be neither an accountant nor a CPA but a management specialist with a brand new Stanford MBA. The MBA described how the firm could help improve the management of the university, and that he had prepared a preliminary consulting contract for my consideration. He then non-too-subtly suggested that a contract with such a prestigious public accounting firm would help make next year's audit more favorable. Realizing now that I had taken the bait and was about to be hooked, I paid for lunch and beat a hasty retreat.

It is common practice, I learned, for accounting firms to turn an annual auditing contract into two or more contracts, one for auditing, another for management advice, and so forth. Accounting professionals insist that there are firewalls between different contracts with the same client, firewalls that guarantee that a management consulting contract could not influence the independence and reliability of an annual audit with the same client. The code of professional ethics of the American Institute of Certified Public Accounts recognizes the possibility of problems here and states that members often serve multiple interests in many different capacities and must demonstrate their objectivity in varying circumstances. The challenge of simultaneously serving multiple interests would certainly be recognized by any serious student of public administration because we, too, serve many interests. But, as Bob Dylan sings, in the end you gotta serve someone.

Serving multiple interests is a real problem in public accounting because it turns out that they make a lot more money on their management and information technology consulting practices than they make doing annual audits.

Public accounting firms clearly trade on their public status and their independent capacity to authenticate the validity of corporate and government accounts. Public governance and oversight systems are controlled by popularly elected executive and legislators. Corporations governance and oversight systems are controlled by corporate boards and by stockholders. Public accounting firms are another matter. They are partnerships without stockholders and without any formalized systems of external oversight or governance. They insist that their peer operated control mechanisms, the Financial Accounting Standards Board and the Auditing Standards Board, are sufficient to look after the interests of the public as against the interests of the accounting firms or their clients. Over the years, even in the face of earlier scandals, the accounting firms battled successfully to stop the development of a formal governmental regulatory body. But, after the Enron and other corporate scandals and the implication of Arthur Andersen LLP in those scandals, Congress moved quickly to take the oversight of public accounting out of the hands of the peers and put it in the hands of the new Public Company Accounting Oversight Board (PCAOB), part of the Securities and Exchange Commission. Members of PCAOB are presently being appointed. Persons under consideration include several distinguished people associated with public administration, including Paul Volcker and Charles Bowsher. One of the leading candidate for chair of the PCAOB was John H. Biggs, a steady voice in favor of increased government oversight of public accounting. Biggs has recently stepped down from chairing the board and serving as chief executive at TIAA-CREF, the huge retirement investment group.

Finally, there is a remarkably tight coupling between accounting firms and universities. The major accounting firms have funded a stunning number of endowed professorships in accounting—there are over 40 Arthur Andersen professors, even more Ernst & Young professors, and an estimate 250 endowed accounting professorates overall. Every prestigious American university has one or more. In research for this piece I discovered that so many of the senior faculty in accounting hold such chairs or have colleagues who hold such chairs that it is difficult to get candid comments about current accounting affairs. It is evident over the years that accounting firms wished to improve accounting education by funding chairs, dissertations and the like. But it is equally evident that by doing so they both enhanced their own status and formed connections that made it difficult to be critical of big time accounting practice. It worked because there is no serious critique of accounting practice. In public administration we have gone through several critiques—the new public administration, the intellectual crisis in public administration, the public choice alternative, reinventing government, and the postmodern critique. There is no such thing in accounting.

It is clear that most public accounting is honest, independent and effective. But it is also clear that the overall arrangements for accounting oversight were weak and that accounting education has not provided the challenging perspectives that all fields of practice need. For public accounting to reposition itself it might ask itself again, what would Arthur Andersen do?

Ethics and Privatization

David Hare's new play *The Permanent Way* is the hottest ticket in London. It is both a documentary and a social commentary on what most British believe to be the disastrous consequences of the privatization of the British railroad system in the Conservative era of Margaret Thatcher and John Major in the 1990s, and into the present Labor administration of Tony Blair.

Convinced that British Rail was overly expensive, poorly managed, undercapitalized, and technologically out of date, the aim of policy makers in the early 1990s was to break it into so many pieces that it could never be put back together again. Although the initial target was to break it into 200 pieces, in the end they settled for 113 buyers. Rolling stock with geographic monopolies went to an assortment of companies, including Richard Branson, the particularly self-confident entrepreneur behind Virgin Air, who famously said, "If you can run one business you can run any business." Train stations were sold to others. The entire track system—the Permanent Way—was sold to a company called Railtrack, which in turn contracted out most of the detailed aspects of track maintenance. Always good for a quote, former Conservative Prime Minister Harold McMillan referred to it as "selling off the family silver."

There were, in a six year period following privatization, four rail disasters that claimed 53 lives and injured hundreds. Based on interviews with the survivors of these disasters, the relatives of those who died, police officials, railroad operators and managers, politicians, and businessmen who were involved, *The Permanent Way* is presented primarily in their words. Because the stage is bare, except for chairs, the audience focuses on the significance of the words. Behind the players who come on and off the stage, the director uses a huge video backdrop showing trains traveling through the British countryside, railway station timetable displays showing the planned routes of the trains that crashed, and finally depictions of high speed train crashes, with rattling sound effects.

The play opens with nine people waiting for a train. It is clear that these are seasoned rail travelers. They talk derisively about how they were once called passengers and are now called customers. They gripe about the overall deterioration of rail services. They complain about the money that was made, and one says, "Warburgs was the bank that handled the privatization of the railways. This man made a fortune—no, I wouldn't say he made a fortune, more John Major walked him into the f@#!ing Bank of England and said, 'take as much as you like. Just take it.'" They rant about the change from experienced railroad engineers to managers and one says, "Wanted: Manager for Sussex County Cricket Club. Interest in cricket not essential." At one point the chief executives of the two largest train companies, Thames and Virgin, had a combined one year of experience in rail management.

The scene then changes to a group of key players in rail privatization including a top official in the Treasury, a senior civil servant, a senior rail executive, an investment banker and an experienced rail engineer. The Treasury official refers to British Rail in the 1980s as a basket case and claims that privatization is the answer. The senior civil servant points out that "the Treasury model for privatization was driven by this rather theoretical view of competition" and "Treasury ideology." The investment banker makes the point that Railtrack bought the permanent way for just under four pounds a share and within two years it was selling for more than 17 pounds a share. The senior rail executive says, "The thing was broken up into 113 pieces, like beads thrown onto a table, all to be held together by local contracts and all in the pursuit of competition. Well, competition in the railways is a great idea in theory, hopeless in practice."

The scenes then turn to bereaved parents, rail police, company employees, the Deputy Prime Minister John Prescott and others. Things move rapidly. Over the course of these scenes we learn that each of the four crashes had to do with the push to cut corners on safety matters so as to make money, to skimp on training, to take risks in the name of efficiency. After each disaster we hear the Deputy Prime Minister say, "This must never happen again. Money is no object in ensuring safety on the railway." Lord Cullen conducted the inquiry into the Ladbroke Grove disaster and referred to it as an accident, enraging one of the bereaved mothers. She said: "Ladbroke Grove wasn't an accident. In the signal box, they admitted, there's an over-ride button you can push and straight away you close down the whole Paddington throat. But of course they don't. They never touch it. My view, they only seem to have two rules on the railway: Never delay the Heathrow Express, it's the golden cash cow; and the second is: Don't kill tourists."

Through the dialogue it becomes evident to the audience that after each disaster there is a formal inquiry headed up by a sir or a lord or some other worthy. In each case they conclude that many different organizations and businesses were involved, that many factors were involved, that rail safety is complex and that every organization involved shares some of the blame. In response one of the lawyers for the bereaved says, "The bereaved know what they want. They want to know that what they have been through will not happen again, and that somebody will be held accountable. These two things." The Deputy Prime Minister, John Prescott, says, "We'll work together. Nobody's to blame."

Among the most difficult challenges associated with disaster is to determine the compensation that should go to the injured and to other survivors and particularly to the bereaved. One bereaved mother says, "When Concorde crashed, every family got a million pounds. In one swoop they got the whole issue out of the way. It is not the money, it's just so you don't have to think about it." The audience learns that settlements ranged from seven thousand to an average of thirty thousand pounds. The audience also learns that during much of this time both Railtrack, which owns the permanent way, and Jarvis, the track maintenance company holding the primary contract, were experiencing record breaking profits. One of the technical directors for Railtrack says, "Oh, it's all about sub-contracting nowadays. And that's bad, they say, because so much can go wrong. Well, we do outsource. We do. But not the important jobs. Not management jobs. We sub-contract labor. I mean, we're not hiring brain surgeons. They're shovel pilots."

Near the end of the play, one of the bereaved mothers sums things up, "I never believed in corruption before. I'm not talking about greased palms, or bribes. I'm talking about the idea of corruption, it being in everyone's interest—the politicians, Railtrack, Jarvis—to do nothing. The response of ordinary people is very different. A group of friends were in a cab traveling to Austen's memorial service, and the driver remarked on the bells pealing out over Trafalgar Square. When he was told they were ringing for someone killed in the Potter's Bar crash, the cab driver turned off his meter. He said, 'It's the least I can do.' They know, you see. People know. The problem with the system is that everyone is able to pass the buck and nobody feels any responsibility."

Many issues of public policy and administration lack intense popular interest. The railways are central to the British way of life and the results of rail privatization are widely understood, which explains the interest in *The Permanent Way*. Not everyone agrees with the anti-privatization perspective in *The Permanent Way*, but everyone agrees it is a powerful evening of theatre.

War and the Uneven Strain

The war with Iraq stimulates this contemplation. Put aside for a moment the big question of whether this is the right war at the right time, and contemplate with me these smaller questions, these public administration questions. Who is fighting this war? Who is paying for this war?

The Rand Corporation is the best source of information on the demographics of the American military, including the active forces, Reserves and National Guard. Rand finds that the primary predictors of a male's (non-officer) military enlistment are that the individual:

- has a low income or his family has low income;
- is unemployed, particularly if he has been unemployed for a year;
- is married, or plans to be married;
- has numerous siblings.

The likelihood of choosing the military over college or work, for male non-officer enlistees, is greater:

- if he is black (20 percent of enlistees vs. 13 percent of age cohort);
- if his mother is working;
- if he has low test scores;
- if one or both of his parents are or have been in the military; and
- if he is poor.

The demographic patterns of female non-officer enlistment are about the same.

Because there has not been a draft for over 30 years, these patterns of non-officer enlistment have resulted in an American military comprised primarily of persons from the low end of the socioeconomic scale. For almost all of these people the military gives them what they need most—steady employment and reliable health care.

This war is not only the job of the regular military, it heavily involves the Reserves and National Guard. Their demographics are relatively similar although they tend to be older (58 percent over age 30) or married (53 percent) and more likely to have children. The enlisted ranks of the Reserves and National Guard come originally from the same pool of enlistees described above. While on active duty each reservist served one or more tours of duty, left the full-time military, took civilian employment and now serves in the Guard or Reserves as a second job. Second jobs are among the most common employment characteristics of those at the lower end of the wage scale.

Although I cannot find a study to prove this assertion, reason suggests that the propensity of low income persons who are married or plan to marry to enlist has a lot to do with health insurance. For those with little education, there are few well-paying jobs with adequate health insurance, and many of the working poor have no coverage (over 40 million). For these people the military is a compelling choice. Reservists retain military health benefits, a critically important hedge against the probability that their primary employer will not provide health coverage.

The answer to the question of who is preparing for war is this: While the vast majority come from the lower end of the socioeconomic scale, the ranks of officers is a different story, but there are eight enlisted persons for every one officer.

Who is paying for this war? The United States is now more financially unequal than at any time since the Depression and the New Deal. We are now the most economically unequal society in the advanced democratic world. The top 20 percent of households earn 56 percent of the nation's income and own an astonishing 83 percent of the nation's wealth. The bottom 40 percent of Americans, where most of the enlisted military come from, earn just 10 percent of the nation's income and control only one percent of its wealth.

So, most of the people in the training camps, on the ships and planes and in the Middle East represent the least advantaged among us.

The good news is that this military is very well trained and equipped, made up of dedicated Americans ready to do whatever is asked of them. What these good Americans are fighting for in Iraq is a big policy question. In democratic government such big questions are answered by our elected officials. But, at the time of this writing, only one of the 535 members of Congress has a child in the enlisted ranks of the military.

As a public administration specialist it is not my place to advise our elected officials on the big question of war. But, as a public administration specialist it is my place to say as boldly as I am able to say it that what we have here is uneven strain. For most of us this war is, at most, an inconvenience and a topic of conversation. We will not be strained at all. But for a few of us, and particularly for a few of the least advantaged of us, this war is a major strain.

How can the strain of a war be evened out? First, there should be more serious consideration of compulsory public service, including service organizations such as Volunteers In Service to America (VISTA). Compulsory service will cause the children of privilege to take up part of the strain. Second, a higher minimum wage and improved health coverage would help the least advantaged of us. Finally, the federal tax code should be altered to even out the strain of paying for this possible war.

As a few of us defend democracy at home and fight for it abroad, it is essential that we remember that fairness and justice are core democratic values. The legitimacy of this war turns, in part, on whether it is waged with an even strain on all Americans.

Original publication dates

Chapters in this publication were originally published as columns in PA TIMES, the monthly newspaper of the American Society for Public Administration

Book Four: Modern Public Organization and Management

Book Five: Public Administration as Reform

Book Six: Public Administration in the Era of Blurred Boundaries

Book Seven: All Public Administration is Local

Index

About the Author

H. George Frederickson is a former president of the American Society for Public Administration. He is Stene Professor of Public Administration at the University of Kansas and co-author of both *The Public Administration Theory Primer* and *The Adapted City: Institutional Dynamics and Structural Change.* E-mail: gfred@ku.edu.